Bulimia:

A Guide to Recovery

Understanding & Overcoming the Binge-Purge Syndrome

Revised Edition

Lindsey Hall
& Leigh Cohn

Gürze Books

Bulimia: A Guide to Recovery
Revised Edition

© 1992 by Lindsey Hall & Leigh Cohn

Gürze Books
P.O. Box 2238
Carlsbad, CA 92018
(619)434-7533

Cover design by Abacus Graphics, Carlsbad, CA
Fabric art by Dorothy Turk

Publishing History:
Copyright ©1992, this book is a fully revised, updated edition of previously published information. The various versions and numbers of copies printed are as follows: *Eating Without Fear* (Bantam Books, 1990) 30,000; *BULIMIA: A Guide to Recovery (Gürze Books, 1986) 21,000;* Set of three booklets (Gürze Books, 1980-83) 15,000.

Library of Congress
Cataloging-in-Publication Data

Hall, Lindsey, 1949-
        Bulimia: a guide to recovery.
        Includes index
1. Bulimia.   2. Eating disorders   3. Psychotherapy.   4. Self-care, health
I. Cohn, Leigh.   II. Title.
ISBN 0-936077-17-4   86-045375

NOTE:
The authors and publisher of this book intend for this publication to provide accurate information. It is sold with the understanding that it is meant to complement, not substitute for, professional medical and/or psychological services.

68097

*Let us all
love and respect
each other
and ourselves.*

Contents

PART II
Overcoming Bulimia

Introduction

I am wide awake and immediately out of bed. I think back to the night before when I made a new list of what I wanted to get done and how I wanted to be. My husband is not far behind me on his way into the bathroom to get ready for work. Maybe I can sneak onto the scale to see what I weigh this morning before he notices me. I am already in my private world. I am overjoyed when the scale says that I stayed the same weight as I was the night before, and I can feel that slightly hungry feeling. Maybe IT will stop today, maybe today everything will change. What were the projects I was going to get done?

We eat the same breakfast, except that I take no butter on my toast, no cream in my coffee and never take seconds (until Doug gets out the door). Today I am going to be really good, which means eating certain predetermined portions of food and not taking one more bite than I think I am allowed. I am careful to see that I don't take more than Doug. I judge by his body. I can feel the tension building. I wish he'd hurry up and leave so I can get going!

As soon as he shuts the door, I try to get involved with one of the myriad of responsibilities on my list. I hate them all! I just want to crawl into a hole. I don't want to do anything. I'd rather eat. I am alone, I am nervous, I am no good, I always do everything wrong anyway, I am not in control, I can't make it through the day, I know it. It has been the same for so long.

I remember the starchy cereal I ate for breakfast. I am into the bathroom and onto the scale. It measures the same, BUT I DON'T WANT TO STAY THE SAME! I want to be thinner! I look in the mirror. I think my thighs are ugly and deformed looking. I see a lumpy, clumsy, pear-shaped wimp. There is always something wrong with what I see. I feel frustrated, trapped in this body, and I don't know what to do about it.

I float to the refrigerator knowing exactly what is inside. I begin with last night's brownies. I always begin with the sweets. At first I try to make it look like nothing is missing, but my appetite is huge and I resolve to make another batch of brownies. I know there is half of a bag of cookies in the trash, thrown out the night before, and I dig them out and polish them off immediately. I take some milk so my vomiting will be smoother. I like the full feeling I get after downing a big glass. I get out six pieces of bread and toast one side in the broiler, turn them over and load them with patties of butter and put them under the broiler again till they are bubbling. I take all six pieces on a plate to the television and go back for a bowl of cereal and a banana. Before the last toast is finished, I am already preparing the next batch of six more pieces. I might have another brownie or five, and a couple of large bowlfuls of ice cream, yogurt or cottage cheese. My stomach is stretched into a huge ball below my ribcage. I know I'll have to go into the bathroom soon, but I want to postpone it. I am in never-never land. I am waiting, feeling the pressure, pacing the floor in and out of rooms. Time is passing. Time is passing. It is almost time.

I wander aimlessly through each of the rooms again, tidying, making the whole house neat and put back together. I finally make the turn into the bathroom. I brace my feet, pull my hair back and stick my finger down my throat, stroking twice. I get up a huge gush of food. Three times, four and another stream of partially-digested food. I can see everything come back. I am glad to see those brownies because they are SO fattening. The rhythm of the emptying is broken and my head is beginning to hurt. I stand up feeling dizzy, empty and weak. The whole episode has taken about an hour.

For nine years, I binged and vomited up to four and five times daily. There were a few days without a binge, but the thoughts were always there, even in my dreams. It was painful and frightening. No one knew about my bulimia, because I kept it safely hidden behind a facade of competence, happiness, and average body weight. When my health and marriage began to fail, however, a series of coincidences brought me face to face with recovery, and I soon became devoted to freeing myself from my obsession with food.

I have not binged for more than a dozen years, but my healing was not an overnight thing. I worked hard and willingly, and underwent an amazing transformation. As the bulimic behavior subsided, I was able to see how it had served me all those years. It was an effective tool for emotional, physical, and spiritual survival when I knew no other; but I wanted to feel at home in my body instead of imprisoned. I purposefully shifted my focus from what I looked like on the outside to what I thought and felt on the inside. In the process, I discovered love and self-esteem at the core of all my thoughts and actions. As a result of the work I have done, I am now confident, healthy, happy, and completely free from bulimia.

In 1980 when my husband, Leigh Cohn, and I wrote my story, *Eat Without Fear,* there were no other publications available on bulimia. The response was tremendous! It inspired and motivated others who were trying to quit; and, as we learned more about the binge-purge syndrome, we realized there was more to tell our audience. Over the next few years, we spoke at colleges around the country, and I became the first person on national television to talk about her own bulimia. We also wrote several books, including *BULIMIA: A Guide to Recovery,* of which there are now more than 75,000 copies in print in various forms. This revised and updated version of *BULIMIA: A Guide to Recovery* is the result of personal experience, years of involvement with this subject, and contact with thousands of bulimics and therapists.

The book is divided into two main parts. The first, "Understanding Bulimia," answers questions often asked about bulimia, and includes my own story, *Eat Without Fear.* The second section, "Overcoming Bulimia," offers motivation, support, inspiration, specific recovery suggestions, things to do instead of bingeing, and advice for loved-ones. "A Two-Week Program to Stop Bingeing" is included here. This is not intended to be a quick cure, but rather an initial experience of self-love to motivate readers to pursue recovery further. Written in a personal, instructive, inspirational tone, the program includes day-by-day activities, exercises, and written assignments. The instructions are direct and specific, but demand attention and dedication. It is followed by "A Guide for Support Groups" which includes agendas and activities for bulimia groups. We have also included resources for further information.

Throughout the book are quotes in italics. These were written by recovered and recovering bulimics and eating disorders therapists who responded to two questionnaires we mailed out in 1983 and 1991. Overall, we received 392 honest and personal impressions on subjects such as: recovering from eating disorders, therapy options, the role of family and friends, and helpful activities in overcoming all kinds of destructive eating. The people who wrote came from diverse backgrounds, and the only apparent element common to all of them was that they had an understanding of bulimia because of their direct experiences with it. They generously shared their insight with us, and we are passing it along to you. The survey is further discussed in the resources chapter.

Much of this book is addressed to "you," readers with bulimia; and, since most bulimics are women, we use feminine pronouns. However, the information and practical self-help tools are equally useful for men. Also, although "I" am the "speaker," Leigh equally contributed to the writing, ideas, and publishing of this effort, and sometimes "we" both speak in the text.

When I first wrote *Eat Without Fear* in 1980, I did so as a way to finalize my involvement with bulimia. I did not expect or intend to become more involved with this subject. However, sharing my experience has remained an integral part of my life, because of the effect it has had on others. Now, Leigh and I work full-time on eating disorders education and publications. We are involved with most of the national organizations dedicated to this field, participate in the annual Eating Disorders Awareness Week, attend national and international conferences on this subject, and continue to write and speak about recovery. We also publish the *Gürze Eating Disorders Bookshelf Catalogue,* which is a comprehensive selection of books and tapes compiled from various sources.

Of all the accomplishments we have achieved, however, nothing compares with the satisfaction of hearing from someone whose recovery has been helped by our words. We hope that they help you.

PART ONE

Understanding Bulimia

CHAPTER 1

Questions Most Often Asked About Bulimia

What is bulimia?

Bulimia is a food obsession characterized by repeated overeating binges followed by purges of forced vomiting, prolonged fasting, excessive exercise, sleeping, or abuse of laxatives, enemas, or diuretics. For an epidemic number of women and men, bulimia is a secret addiction that dominates their thoughts, severely undercuts their self-esteem, and actually threatens their lives. The symptoms are described by the Egyptians, and in the Hebrew Talmud; and, bulimia (Greek for "ox-hunger") was widely practiced during Greek and Roman times. It has also been called bulimia nervosa and bulimarexia.

In 1980, the American Psychiatric Association formally recognized bulimia in its third edition of *Diagnostic and Statistical Manual of Mental Disorders*. The criteria was revised in 1987:*

A. Recurrent episodes of binge eating (rapid consumption of a large amount in a discrete period of time, usually less than two hours).

B. A feeling of lack of control over eating behavior during the eating binges.

---

* The American Psychiatric Association, Washington, D.C., 1980, 1987.

C. The person regularly engages in either self-induced vomiting, strict dieting or fasting, or vigorous exercise in order to prevent weight-gain.

D. A minimum average of two binge eating episodes a week for at least three months.

E. Persistent over concern with body shape and weight.

Most bulimics are women, but it is difficult to say how many people have bulimia. Statistics may not truly reflect the total numbers because bulimics are generally secretive about their behavior. In fact, college students have answered questionnaires more truthfully when told to put a dab of their saliva on the survey paper, because they believed it could be chemically analyzed to determine if they were bulimic! Of the hundreds of studies done on the prevalence of eating disorders, the most reliable statistics indicate that about 8% of women and 1% of men meet the clinical criteria for bulimia.* However, some studies offer much higher numbers; and, some reports suggest that as many as one of every three college-aged women have engaged in bulimia, without strictly meeting the diagnostic criteria. Whatever the actual figures, there are a tremendous number of bulimic women and a significant number of men.

Let me add here that judging someone with an eating disorder as wasteful, self-centered and spoiled, invalidates that person's feelings, ignores underlying issues and increases the individual's shame. It is time we understood that an eating disorder is not just about food.

---

* *The Etiology of Bulimia Nervosa,* Craig Johnson & Mary E. Connors; Basic Books, New York, c. 1987.

Why do people become bulimic?

There is no easy answer. Just as the life of every individual is unique, so are the reasons why they became bulimic and the paths they must take to overcome it.

Bulimia is generally considered to be a psychological and emotional disorder, but there are significant studies that claim bulimia is related to major affective disorder, and might be caused by heredity and chemical imbalances in the body. (See "Can I take a drug to get better?" in this chapter.) In some cases, therefore, medication will alleviate the binge-purge behavior or the blanket of depression. However, the underlying reasons most people give for their bulimia are a complex mix of low self-esteem, childhood conflicts and cultural pressures.

People become addicted to avoid painful feelings—past as well as present. Some of these feelings have their origins in childhood, such as feeling unloved and unlovable, ashamed, afraid, or incompetent. Others may come from the pressure to conform or to be accepted by peers. Most devastating of all are the feelings associated with low self-esteem—that we have no worth, that our lives have no value or purpose, and that we will never be fulfilled or happy.

Paradoxically, bulimia in the early stages will raise self-esteem when it provides someone with a way to be successful, in this case at achieving the cultural ideal of thinness. Indeed, many individuals turn to purging when they have failed at a diet, and are faced with the fear that there is no other way for them to lose weight. Once the bingeing and purging cycle begins, however, the resulting metabolic imbalances and habitual escape become an ever-deepening pit, eventually eroding any initial sense of self-worth and control. It is also important to note that the rewards for thinness are only implied, and although diets and a smaller body promise a happier life, they rarely deliver.

The question remains as to why bulimia is the chosen escape. There appear to be similarities in the backgrounds, personalities and experiences of eating disordered individuals which will help clarify this. All of these will not apply to every case, but certainly some will.

Most bulimics come from dysfunctional families in which the emotional, physical, or spiritual needs of family members are not met. In many of these households, feelings are not verbally expressed. There may be a history of depression, alcoholism, drug abuse, or eating disorders; and, the child might unconsciously recognize that escape is an appropriate thing to do. In this context, food becomes a "good girl's" drug, something which does not have the negative connotations of alcohol or drug abuse.

Bulimics are often considered "ideal" children, and will go out of their way to be "people pleasers." They present an acceptable facade—seeming outgoing, confident, and independent—while anxious feelings bubble underneath. They may be valued for not needing to be nurtured, for taking care of themselves, and for growing up early. Bulimia can be a seemingly innocuous way of expressing what cannot be said directly, such as, "I want to be taken care of," or "Will you love me as I am?"

Sometimes, people use bulimia to postpone growing up. The child who has looked to others for validation and feelings of self-worth and who has assumed a "perfect little girl" role because it works at home may experience tremendous fear at having to trust herself and face the outside world alone. This insecurity is sometimes unconsciously reinforced by parents who also do not want to let go, or who have related to their children within the confines of a role and not as individuals.

Too often, parents fall into roles as well, limiting the relationships and personal growth within the family. Mothers may reinforce the idea that it is important for women to be thin. Fathers may be relegated to the role of economic provider and disciplinarian rather than taking part in the emotional life of the family. Girls in particular can develop insecurities about their appearance, competence, and ability to be loved if they are not valued for their own unique strengths. In a society where roles for women are changing, strong relationships with parents of both sexes based on the child's uniqueness will give him or her the confidence and ability to make smart decisions and negotiate healthy relationships in the future.

Bulimics tend to be overly judgmental of themselves and others, have difficulty expressing emotions through language, fear criticism, avoid disagreements, and have low self-esteem— all traits which make having relationships with others difficult. In fact, many people in our survey indicated that they were uncomfortable with intimate relationships, and that the bulimia was their predictable, reliable, unquestioning ally. Many had been sexually or emotionally abused as children and had difficulty trusting others. In this way, the bulimic rituals and thoughts protected them from what might be rejection, abandonment, or other potential pain. However, it also prevented them from experiencing any love, which was described on one woman's survey as "The Great Filler." The bulimia thus became her only relationship, albeit an empty one.

The bulimics from our survey identified various causes for their bulimia. Many remembered specific reasons for their initial binges, as well as how the behavior subsequently served them. Few women thought it would become addictive. In addition to the original causes, which still existed, they were faced with guilt, secrecy, physical side-effects, and an increasing number of reasons to use bulimia. Frequently mentioned were: boredom, the influences of media and culture, family dynamics, mental "numbness," the taste of food, a failed diet, death of a loved one, and sexual tension.

Most bulimics have been preoccupied with eating and diet for years, but the initial binge-purge episodes might be triggered by specific events, such as: traumatic change (graduation, moving away from home, marriage, etc.), unresolved grief, career changes, a failed diet, and rejection by a lover or wished-for lover. These survey comments were among the several specific reasons offered for starting the bulimic behavior:

I started because I was rejected by a boy at age fifteen. Since I liked myself, I really felt the only thing wrong with me was my weight.

I first developed my eating disorder the night before my first college finals. My father had passed away a month earlier, and I was nervous about finals and about returning home and having him not be there.

I had been dieting for a couple of weeks, and was getting tired of it.

I never thought about trying it until I read about it.

I started throwing up binges during my fourth month of pregnancy, when I could not handle my changing body and dieting away the calories became impossible.

No matter what the underlying reasons for choosing bulimia as a method of coping with painful feelings, the fact is that bulimia works on many different levels. Binge-eating provides instant relief. The mind ceases to dwell on anything but food and how to get it down. It replaces all other actions, thoughts, and emotions. Even vomiting can be pleasurable when it is the most intimate contact we allow with our own bodies. When the whole binge-purge episode is over, for a brief moment, the bulimic regains control. No longer feeling guilty for having eaten so many calories, she is drained, relaxed, and high.

Since bulimia is falsely perceived as less dangerous than alcoholism or drug abuse, it is especially insidious and captivating. Food is always available for a "fix," and eating in public, even if on the run, is accepted and not unusual. There is also nothing to give a bulimic away, because her weight usually appears close to normal. Food gives life, it heals, nurtures, and means love. The safety, relief, availability, pleasure, and companionship represented by food far outweigh any immediate drawbacks. It is a short-term solution for life-long stress.

Why are bulimics mainly women?

In the most simple terms, we live in a society which is fundamentally unsatisfying to many women, and eating disorders are a symbol of this inner emptiness.

While it is true that men and women are naturally concerned with attraction, along the path through childhood, adolescence, and adulthood, women constantly get the message that how they look is more important than what they think, do, or feel. Particularly when they turn the corner into puberty, moving away from their families to face the culture at large, young girls are bombarded with images of female bodies as objects which are scrutinized and judged unmercifully. They are also aware of stereotypically termed "feminine" traits, such as cleanliness, docility, unselfishness, politeness, and sometimes being a tease.

By the time sexual game-playing starts, most of them already know that their bodies are tools for popularity and power, and that there is appropriate and inappropriate behavior associated with being a girl. It is this role within this society which is at different times limiting, confusing, frightening, and unfulfilling, propelling enormous numbers of women into the safety and numbness of food problems.

• Having a female body in this society can be frightening.

Men are more sexually driven than women, anthropologically and socially. Women, on the other hand, are driven more by a deep desire for connection and a willingness to please others. These two factors have created an environment of pervasive sexual abuse and harassment against women within our society, which we are just beginning to face. We have been in denial about it for a long time.

Recent statistics of sexual abuse and violence against women are staggeringly high. An eating disorder is a way of taking back control, of saying, "My body is my own. I am in control of what goes in and out of it." It can be an unconscious re-enactment of the original abuse or a way to punish the body which was "to blame" for the assault. Ultimately, an eating disorder is a safe place to hide from the pain and fear of mistreatment.

• Women tend to have lower self-esteem than men.

When young girls turn the corner into puberty, a strange thing often happens. The sure sense of self, strong opinions, and unabashed involvement, give way to powerlessness, insecurity, and doubts about their appearance. They are no longer cute little girls, they are budding sexual women. From a girl's perspective, this puts her in a vulnerable position with men, and a competitive one with other women. In an effort to please everyone, she loses the connection to herself. Low self-esteem is the result.

Having a "perfect" body has become a panacea for this low self-esteem. Outer, rather than inner beauty, is the measure of worth. Although the cultural ideal has changed from one decade to the next, there has always been a standard to which women have compared themselves. The implied rewards to a particular "look" are not insignificant either. The long, lean, and clean bodies of today are falsely equated with great sex, happiness, marriage, feelings of self-worth, willpower, independence, fulfillment, success, and an overall glamorous life. Consequently, many women develop eating disorders when they have been unable to diet successfully and are faced with the fear of getting fat in a society that discriminates against large female bodies.

• Contemporary society denies the natural variety and function of women's bodies.

"Becoming a woman" is for many an embarrassing, self-conscious affair, requiring daily self-scrutiny. Most feel required to shave their legs and underarms, hide their periods, and control body odors. Even women who have experienced the miracle of giving birth are driven to flatten their stomachs afterwards, as though it had never happened!

Denying women's deepest biological truth—that they are in effect co-creators of life itself—trivializes their lives. An eating disorder can ease the pain of being disconnected from this inner source of strength and meaning.

• Women are expected to act in a "ladylike" way.

Not only are there standards for how women should look, there are narrow limits to what is stereotypically termed "ladylike" behavior. As females, we are expected to keep the anger in check, not assert our needs, not even talk too much! Consequently, many of us have little experience with our emotions or appetites for sex, food, or living.

Many women with bulimia report fearing the intensity of these bottled-up feelings. Letting them out would mean being engulfed by them or engulfing others. Some say that they cannot distinguish one feeling from another, or that they swing back and forth from extreme highs to lows. Controlling their bodies, specifically food intake, becomes a concrete way to feel in control of this inner instability. Thinness becomes a measure of emotional control, and bulimia a way to insure it.

• It is frustrating to be a woman in the work place.

Although the women's movement did provide opportunities for some women who took advantage, today the majority of working women continue to be discriminated against in the male-dominated marketplace and political arena. Those women who are able to land creative jobs in the areas of their interest and expertise are often paid less than men and are under tremendous pressure to perform. Bulimia can be a symptom of a life devoid of meaning or material rewards. It can help let off steam, or provide a way to self-sabotage in order to avoid failure or close working relationships.

• The media perpetuates the status quo.

It is important to mention the broad influence of the media. Images of women as sexual objects are endlessly reinforced via television, movies, magazines, newspapers, and consumer products, conveying to both sexes that women should be thin, pretty, and sexy. While a cover girl's photo or ice cream advertisement does not cause a binge, these constant reminders that thinner equals better establishes values that lead to distorted ways of viewing food and the self. Ironically, many of the thin actresses and models, who are paid enormous sums for their "look" and skinny bodies, are themselves struggling with eating disorders in an effort to remain marketable.

What are the special issues faced by men with bulimia?

The actual numbers of men with bulimia are unknown and are certainly less than for women, but it is likely that more men have bulimia than anyone thought in the early 80s, when information about this eating disorder first emerged. In fact, one researcher found twice as many college-aged men reporting bulimic symptoms in 1983 than in 1980. However, much of the latest research on this subject is based on small studies and lacks conclusive findings.

Considering the issues that surround bulimia, such as guilt, shame, and low self-esteem, it is understandable that men might feel these emotions even more intensely when they have what has been generally regarded as a "women's" disease. For this reason, many bulimic men may have been reluctant to seek professional help. Some, who are using exercise addiction as a type of purge, will deny that they have a problem with food.

For the most part, it appears that men become bulimic for the same kinds of reasons that women do. As mentioned earlier, some male athletes, such as wrestlers and gymnasts, use bulimia to maintain or lose weight, as is the case for female athletes. Some people suggest that more women are bulimic than men because society has traditionally placed more of an emphasis on women's appearance; but, men are increasingly encouraged to conform to a narrow range of body types. Heavy male models are as rare as full-figured females.

Men are under particular pressure to appear strong, in control, and independent. Many have difficulty expressing feelings and have had little experience in emotionally intimate relationships. Few would want to be labelled obsessed with their appearance. All these traits might make them more susceptible to turning to bulimia as a coping mechanism, as well as extremely reluctant to seek help.

In general, however, most research concludes that there are far more similarities than differences when comparing men and women with bulimia. In addition to diet-consciousness, other factors such as dysfunctional families, sexual abuse, low self-esteem, and lack of meaning in one's life will contribute to the causes for becoming bulimic, regardless of sex. Recovery outcomes for each are also parallel.

Finding adequate therapy has its own unique concerns for men. Treatment options for women are plentiful and diverse, but there are not many programs available solely for men with bulimia. Therefore, finding professional support may require a lot of searching and may mean settling for a general men's or mixed bulimia support group. Men might find it necessary to step outside the roles they've defined for themselves, and to interpret feminist recovery literature to meet their own needs. As a society, both men and women perpetuate negative stereotypes, and it is up to both sexes to learn how to relate to each other in fulfilling, nurturing ways. As you know, the language of this book primarily addresses women, but the underlying messages and suggested activities are also worthwhile for men.

How is bulimia related to sexual trauma?

Most clinical studies indicate that roughly 60% of eating disorders patients report having been sexually abused. However, that figure does not include individuals who have repressed the memories of their abuse, so the actual figures are undoubtedly higher. An eating disorder appears to be a highly-effective way for someone who has been sexually abused to protect herself both physically and emotionally.

It is important to be aware of the extremely sensitive nature of this topic, and that a self-help book such as this is not adequate "therapy" for healing these issues. With the understanding that victims need to work with a qualified therapist who has experience treating individuals suffering with both eating disorders and sexual trauma, I will present an overview on this subject. Also, although I am using the pronoun "she," incest and sexual abuse occurs with startlingly high incidence among males, with similar consequences.

Being sexually assaulted, especially by a "trusted" adult, parent, or sibling, is a terrifying, confusing, horrific experience for anyone, especially a young child. It is an act of violence and betrayal so intense that just remembering it is agonizingly painful. In order to survive not only the trauma itself, but also the memory of it, a child will dissociate from the event and from those parts of herself which were present at that time. She may even consider the person being raped to be separate from herself, because the pain is too much for her to bear. Her emotional and physical survival depend on her *not* remembering the events or her feelings connected with what happened.

An eating disorder is a highly-effective way to protect, repress, complete, divert, numb or confuse these feelings and memories. Since it is not within a child's realm of possibility to blame the abuser for what happened, her body becomes the focus for hatred and control. Stuffing down food will stuff down the anger, and silence the voice that cries out, "Don't do this to me!" Planning and executing a binge will numb anxieties and deny physical needs, such as hunger or affection. Being in charge of what does and does not go into the body is a way to symbolically regain that control which was absent during the original trauma.

The relationship with the food makes it difficult to have full relationships with others, thus eliminating the risk of another betrayal. Depending on the individual's internal survival tools, being extremely large or thin, or even *perceiving* one's self as too large or too thin, is a way of keeping potential abusers at a distance. Finally, the painful and violent act of vomiting is a way of expressing and releasing rage and self-loathing.

Many victims become promiscuous, masochistic or even fantasize about rape during consenting lovemaking without realizing that they are hooked on the "high" of relief they experienced blocking out their assault. Likewise, they can repeat this "forbidden high" by bingeing and purging. Some bulimics compulsively follow rituals, which might mirror repeated incidents, such as molestation from a baby-sitter every Saturday night or visits from a sibling when parents are out of the house. Forced eating and vomiting also parallels the act of forced oral sex. These repetitive behaviors may be an attempt on the part of the unconscious to complete the original abuse in the present. An even more upsetting eating pattern may be the result of Satanic rituals, which could involve swallowing excrement or blood. Given the appalling scope of sexual trauma within this context, it is apparent that an eating disorder can be a crucial mechanism for survival.

Although we are defining sexual abuse here in terms of more extreme behaviors, virtually every woman has suffered sexual humiliation in some form or another. Their breasts have been "accidentally" brushed up against, their virginity has been the subject of male gossip, and they have been whistled or jeered at by strangers. In all of these cases, it is the girl/woman who is erroneously victimized by the standard line, "She was asking for *it.*" It is no coincidence that epidemic numbers of women also suffer from some type of food/weight conflict. It is a sad commentary on Western civilization that women's bodies have become their enemies, instead of the natural wonder that they are.

Sexual trauma must be treated in a safe, trusted environment. Breaking through repressed memories and returning the inner child to an experience of unconditional love and acceptance is a tremendous undertaking. It requires gentle understanding and patience by therapist and patient alike. Keep in mind that eliminating the binge-purge behavior without introducing healthy coping skills can result in a reliving of the original horror. Coming to terms with the nightmare that lies beneath the bulimic surface is best achieved with the guidance of a trained and skilled professional.*

Because of the sexual abuse, I had an overwhelming feeling of loathing and distrust of my body. I used food to avoid, and numb the feelings of pain, rage, helplessness, and hatred that were triggered along with body memories. Food gave me a misguided sense that at last I could be in charge of what went in and out of my body.

Working and uncovering the truth about my family, and the fact that I was incested, helped everything make sense. I saw how

---

* Much of the information in this section was taken from talks by Mark F. Schwartz, Sc.D., Director of the Masters and Johnson Sexual Trauma Programs.

wounded I was, and how much pain and anger I worked dutifully to deny. I began to see that I had value, and that I was lovable and competent, but that I had not been treated that way by my parents. I realized that my eating disorder was motivated by my archaic need to protect my family, and that I was actually recreating my abuse.

When I was 12, my brother began sexually abusing me. I was overwhelmed with confusion, and believed if I became fat, he might leave me alone. I think gaining 40 pounds in three months was also my way of saying, "Hey, there's something wrong here," without having to verbalize it.

When growing up, my parents were unable to be emotionally available to me, due to marital conflicts, depression, and alcohol. The physical and sexual abuse began at an early age. Much of the abuse centered around food, with my father demanding favors for desserts. Some days, it was all right to leave food on my plate, others it wasn't and I'd sit into the early morning hours, while Dad added extra portions of my least favorite foods. Food became my lasting enemy.

I had a swallowing problem, due to being forced into oral sex. I would spit out all of my food, even liquids. I had been through every medical test in the book, because the doctors thought there was something wrong with my throat. After four years of therapy, that problem is finally gone; but, it comes back at times of high stress or when memories surface.

It's important for parents, therapists, doctors, and the public to know that women who were sexually abused tend to have eating disorders. It's a way of dealing with all of the feelings you have inside—rage, anger, secrecy, betrayal, and powerlessness. An eating disorder is a feeling disorder.

How does bulimia affect my relationships?

Bulimia is sometimes referred to as a relationship disorder because it is, to a large degree, the result of beliefs about the self which are born in our most important relationships. It is a protective device which insures that past hurts are not remembered or repeated in the present.

As children, the ways in which we are treated by our parents, other adults, and peers, tell us something about our significance, competence, and ability to be loved. Unfortunately, many of us have been abused emotionally and physically by the very people entrusted with our lives. With our child's mind, we cannot believe that the fault lies with our caretakers, so we blame ourselves.

This is not to imply that eating disorders develop only in households where there is extreme violence or abuse. Being repeatedly ignored or undervalued can be as damaging to a child's self-image as being incested. Children who do not feel loved or safe in any type of family don't trust their own actions. They will then look outside themselves for cues on how to behave. As a result, their relationships will be other-directed and founded in low self-esteem.

Bulimia, which often begins as an innocent attempt to maintain thinness and thus please others, is an example of this other-directed behavior. However, over time, it becomes more like a coat of armor walling off the pain of neglect, abuse, and shame. While it appears to be protecting the individual within by preserving a false front, it is also an effective way to keep people at a distance. Bulimics interact with people only to the degree that they feel safe, knowing that they can withdraw at any time to their familiar, repetitive behaviors. Even when a bulimic appears to be present in conversation, her mind can be light years away in the last or next binge.

Certain aspects of bulimia are particularly detrimental to forming honest, fulfilling relationships. Obviously, maintaining a happy, competent facade on the outside while feeling anxious or depressed on the inside is an effort and a distraction. The binge and purge behaviors are done in secret, usually surrounded by feelings of guilt and shame. Mood swings and lying are common characteristics. Stealing, which was mentioned by close to 40% of the people who answered our survey, reinforces low self-esteem and hiding. Focussing on thinness encourages competition between women instead of support, and emphasizes the sexual nature of relationships with men instead of affection or respect.

Over time, a bulimic's relationship with food will come to supersede all other relationships. As one person who responded to our survey said, "Bulimia is a friend who does not criticize, judge, compete or reject." However, bulimic behavior cannot love us the way we need to be loved. It does not nurture, support, or fulfill us as anyone who has gorged and purged themselves over and over will testify. It is a tenuous short-term solution for buried long-term pain, creating loneliness and isolation in its wake.

Giving up bulimic behavior is extremely frightening for someone who has little experience being close to others. It means risking rejection and facing feelings of worthlessness; but, the payoffs are honesty, trust, intimacy, and love. As the section in this book on getting support emphasizes, an open, trusting relationship with even one person is a crucial factor in recovery. Many people found this trust in therapy, others found it with parents, lovers, spouses, and friends.

The very nature of an eating disorder prevents the development of relationships. How could I have a relationship with someone based on honesty and truth if I was constantly lying about how much I ate, didn't eat, exercised, or purged?

When I am in love or working on intimacy, my eating habits normalize, but when I have no close relationships or involvement with others, I feel like I am starving. Food reduces the anxiety, and masks the feelings. Only working on intimacy stops this pattern. For me, relationship-building is essential to recovery.

Basically, my life became a massive cover-up. Any lie or deception that protected my freedom to binge-purge was okay, and I'd always placed a high value on honesty prior to this! My relationships with my family members deteriorated as they caught me in numerous lies. They couldn't trust most of what I said. I actually believed that the reason my sisters were tracking me around the house, in an attempt to stop my vomiting, was because they were jealous that I was finally thinner than they were!

When I went out with friends, I was so detached from what was going on that all I could do was calculate how fast I needed to get to the bathroom to vomit. I had no real interest in the people around me; but, through therapy, that's all changing now.

I recall on many occasions, turning on my answering machine, settling down to plates and plates of my favorite binge foods, and listening to friends leave messages while I frantically shoveled food into my mouth. Food had become more important than my friends. Food was my BEST friend.

I am listening to others now. Before I thought only I was right.

As I became more comfortable with myself, I saw my life change in many ways. I found myself surrounded by friends who really liked me. And they were happy people, not miserable and depressed like my old friends. I have learned how to say "no" to people, and earned a lot of respect for doing so.

Is it the same as anorexia nervosa?

For many years bulimia was considered to be one type of anorexic behavior. By recognizing bulimia as a separate disorder in DSM-III, the American Psychiatric Association isolated a much larger group than those who could be clinically classified as strictly anorexic. In both cases, the relationship with food is a symptom of other serious problems.

Although anorexics also purge, anorexia nervosa is characterized by self-starvation; and, the clinical diagnosis includes the loss of 25% of body weight. However, in general, anorexics reject food, have lower body weight, are younger, and are socially and sexually less mature. In contrast, the majority of bulimics' weight appear closer to normal, most began purging in their late teens or early twenties (many anorexics turn to bulimia), and are more socially outgoing. Hospitalization is often necessary for anorexics, who have a high fatality rate—10-15% of anorexics die from the disease. There is no definitive data for bulimia fatality statistics, but the clinical impression is that they are low, and definitely not as high as for anorexia nervosa. Eating and vomiting was easier for me than starving, so I was never anorexic. I sometimes wished for the power to starve, but I never could!

There are, as I mentioned above, basic similarities in the issues underlying anorexia nervosa and bulimia which have translated into their shared concern with the size of their bodies and what they have or have not eaten. Obviously, both are focused on an inner empty place, which can be viewed in physical, emotional or spiritual terms. Both use food to handle intense feelings of different kinds, such as depression, anger, rejection, loneliness, selfishness, fear of independence or dependence, and love. Both also use food to avoid situations where there is a potential for conflict, disapproval or failure. Certainly, both use food to express something that they feel is unacceptable or they are unable to express directly.

However, while a binge and purge can give a bulimic the courage to face the world, it is not eating which is empowering to an anorexic. Although some anorexics do engage in purges if they eat more than they consider safe, not eating remains their primary tool for self-preservation. It would appear that recovery for these individuals is less a matter of avoiding a binge than it is eating enough to be healthy, but actually the bottom line for both remains to be able and willing to care for themselves with appropriate amounts of food (not starving or stuffing) in a healthy, self-nurturing way.

What is a typical binge?

"Typical" depends entirely on the individual. The size and frequency can vary as well as the type of purge and the length of time between sessions. A binge is really whatever the person feels guilty about—one woman considered a single can of diet soda to be too much. However, many bulimics have said that they can "relate to" my binges, which I've described in the Introduction.

Frequently I started a binge while in the course of eating what I thought to be a "good" or "safe" meal. For example, I may have gone to a salad bar and carefully allowed myself a moderate portion. As I ate the salad, I began to feel guilty about the calories in the salad dressing or the fact that I had taken croutons. At one point in the meal, I decided I had eaten one bite too many. Rather than stop eating, I'd think, "What's the difference. I've already gone too far. I'll do a binge, and none of the calories will matter after I vomit."

If I had my choice, I would eat sweets and refined carbohydrates. A single binge might include: a quart of ice cream, a bag of cookies, a couple of batches of brownies, a dozen donuts, and a few candy bars. When I was desperate, I would binge on anything: oatmeal, cottage cheese, carrots, or day-old rolls that I fished out of the trash from what was to be my last-ever binge.

My stomach stretched so much that I looked pregnant, and I usually postponed vomiting for about 30 minutes of numbness. Then I'd stick my fingers down my throat until I had vomited everything that would come up. The whole episode lasted about an hour, and I often felt very weak and dizzy afterwards. I did not abuse laxatives, enemas, or diuretics, although others with bulimia do.

Is it dangerous?

Absolutely! Excessive vomiting can cause death from cardiac arrest, kidney failure, heart arrhythmia due to electrolyte imbalance, or severe dehydration. Other serious physical side-effects include rotten teeth, digestive disorders, amenorrhea, malnutrition, anemia, infected glands, blisters in the throat, internal bleeding, hypoglycemia, icy hands and feet, and a ruptured stomach or esophagus. Some people use syrup of Ipecac, detergents, or even pencils to induce vomiting. These "aids" are extremely dangerous as well.

Laxative abuse can irritate intestinal nerve endings, which can inhibit them from triggering contractions. Heavy use of laxatives or enemas removes protective mucus from the intestinal lining, which can result in bowel infections. The lower bowel can lose muscle tone, becoming limp and unable to produce contractions. Dehydration and fluid imbalances can occur with the same side-effects as listed above. Also, laxative abusers often have rectal pain, gas, constipation, diarrhea (or both), and bowel tumors.

There are devastating emotional side-effects to bulimia, as well. Although it is an effective way to avoid problems, it solves none. What's more, it brings with it a whole new set of complications which can mask the old ones, or make them worse. For example, a person who is afraid of others may use bulimia to keep her distance by hiding her embarrassing thoughts and rituals. Or someone who feels incompetent may perfect the art of throwing up, while attempting little else. In this way, whatever precipitated the binge-purge behavior is effectively denied, and in the long run, buried beneath fresh shame and guilt.

What does it feel like to binge-vomit?

In answering this question, it is important to remember that bulimia serves a purpose for the person using it. In other words, they would not be binge eating and purging if it made them feel worse rather than better. Particularly in the early stages, when purging is excused as a way to lose or maintain low weight, bulimia provides a false sense of self-esteem, competence and control. In the later stages, giving it up means facing the very reasons why we had no self-esteem, why we felt incompetent and why we are terrified of being out of control. Obviously, once begun, it feels better to do it than not.

The mental "numbness" and physical "high" are important reasons that the binge-vomiting behavior itself becomes so addictive. In fact, many women from our survey who were addictive. In fact, many women from our survey who were compulsive about food were also alcoholics, or came from families where substance abuse existed. Bingeing temporarily removes stress, like a drug. All focus is on the cycle, from trying to avoid a binge, giving in to the urge, planning, and execution. After a vomiting purge, there is also a physical "high" from the pressure of being upside down, and exhausting physical effort. There may be sexual feelings from the emerging, private excitement, complete involvement, fullness, stroking, and sudden release.

In my case, in the calm after the purging storm, I promised myself that I would never binge again, adding feelings of hope and renewal to the cycle. But shortly thereafter, I always started anew. For more than five years, I binged and vomited four or five times—and more—practically every day. Several surveyed women commented about the drug-like aspect of bulimia:

I can easily see how, during stressful times of your life, you seek some kind of comfort. I found this in food. Others find it in drugs and alcohol.

I like the high and then the numbness.

When I first tried to give up my bulimic behaviors, I began to drink more alcohol. I was substituting one escape for another. I would get so depressed over my drinking that I would finally binge. I have now joined Alcoholics Anonymous, have been sober five months, and find my bulimia much more manageable. I am now recovered, but until I quit drinking I kept having recurrent episodes of my old bulimic behavior.

I don't binge when I start drinking alcohol. I am afraid if I keep this up, I might become an alcoholic.

Before I started therapy, I never associated my desire to binge with my emotions. I always felt it was an uncontrollable desire for huge amounts of food. Now I understand the binge takes the place of allowing myself to feel any emotions.

No matter how down and depressed you feel, think of food as a temporary filling or "high." Find something permanent, because after you purge, you'll feel the same or even worse. Why waste your time?

Do bulimics share other behaviors besides overeating and purging?

People with eating disorders have compulsive personalities; the rituals they create are safe and familiar places to reside. Many of their rituals revolve around food and body image, such as arranging food on their plates, excessive exercise, eating systematically, looking in the mirror, and obsessive calorie counting. Some behaviors are not related to food, such as always knowing where the nearest bathroom is, lying, keeping secrets, and kleptomania.

Most bulimics take exhaustive steps to cover up their bingeing. During the five years of my first marriage, my husband never found out about my closely-guarded secrets. No one knew! Covering my tracks was part of my daily routine. Lying about food was second nature to me. For example, if I went to the same grocery two days in a row to buy large quantities of binge food, I would tell the checkers that I was a nursery school teacher buying snacks for the children. My rituals included a preoccupation with scales, mirrors, and trying on clothes. I used to weigh myself before and after binges to be sure that I gained no weight. (At one point in my recovery, I took a hammer to the scale!) I could not pass a mirror without judging every slight bulge or hair out of place.

In our survey, 37% of the bulimics mentioned kleptomania. Eating binges can get quite expensive, and one way to offset the cost of food is to steal it! I shoplifted food, but stopped when I got caught with a container of artificial sweetener. However, there is certainly more to kleptomania than just basic economics. In my case, I felt unworthy and incapable of affording "nice" things, although I spent vast amounts on food. I wanted love and attention; and, not knowing how to get those emotional rewards, I settled for the temporary satisfaction of new things. Sometimes I just wanted the rush of doing something I shouldn't. The women in our survey had similar experiences. Their stealing ranged from candy bars to larger, more expensive items. Most of those who stole also indicated that it was not too difficult a pattern to change. A few women were arrested, then stopped immediately, such as this one:

I stopped stealing after I got caught with a chicken in my purse!

How do I know if I have it?

Have we been talking about you? I binged and vomited daily for nine years without thinking I had a problem. When I read a magazine article about bulimia, I became aware for the first time that there were other people who had the same eating behavior as mine.

Bulimics can become addicted to the gorge-purge syndrome on a daily basis, or can continue with occasional binges for many years. Whether you binge and force yourself to vomit daily or only on weekends, you are still abusing your body. Even if you are obsessive only in your thoughts about weight, diet, and food, you have a food problem, although maybe not the clinical definition of bulimia. I know of no one who does not enjoy an occasional large meal (holiday binges!), but an obsession is an escape. If you have food obsessions, you have a problem, regardless of its name.

How long does it take to get better?

That's up to you. The behavior does not suddenly stop without an effort. In fact, it is addictive enough to continue as a life-long obsession. I have corresponded with a woman in her sixties who has been bulimic for more than forty years! In the past, so little was known about bulimia that people commonly continued for years before seeking help. Now, there are national and local organizations, treatment facilities, private therapists, support groups, and books solely devoted to eating disorders.

There are a few necessary steps to recovery. The first is acknowledging that you have a problem and making the decision to change. For some people, prolonged therapy, or even hospitalization, is necessary. Generally, overcoming bulimia takes time and a firm commitment, and increased effort and determination will make it happen faster.

The time it takes to stop the bingeing behavior varies with each individual. I have heard of people who have gone "cold turkey," stopping instantly, and of others who have decreased the number of binges slowly over a period of years while they worked on the underlying issues. Stopping the binge-purge behavior is like opening Pandora's box. Within are the reasons why the bulimia began and took hold, and these need to be faced.

I am often asked how long it took me to recover. I spent a year and a half working to stop the binge-purge behavior. There was a time when only one binge each day seemed like an impossible goal, but days extended into weeks, and eventually my goals were to not binge for a month. Now, I find it somewhat difficult to even remember my struggle with bulimia. I have not binged for well over a decade, and I do not think about returning to it. There are times, especially during menstruation, when I crave and eat more food than usual, especially chocolate. This increase is nothing like the eating binges when I was bulimic, either in content or quality. Ridding myself of the obsessive thoughts about food and my body took longer because I had to confront the issues that led me to become bulimic in the first place. It was three or four years before I considered myself completely "cured."

Not everyone agrees that you can be "cured." Some experts believe that bulimia is an addiction and that abstinence is the only way to prevent future relapse. They stress the addictive nature of certain types of foods which trigger responses that lead to bingeing. Like alcoholism, a complete cure is not possible because you will always be prone to bulimia, even if you do not practice the binge-purge behavior again. They would say that you are always in recovery.

I share the point-of-view of experts who believe in "legalizing" food. Identifying certain foods as "good" or "bad" gives them power and focus. Instead of restricting, advocates of this approach stress differentiating stomach hunger from emotional hunger, and the importance of getting satisfaction from eating what your body wants. They take the emphasis away from food, and suggest that when a preoccupation with eating and weight ends, bingeing stops as well.

In spite of my personal experience, I recommend many therapists and facilities who promote the abstinence approach, as well as those who do not. The information in this book applies to bulimics interested in recovery regardless of their stance on this issue. I do not advocate any specific modality of treatment—whatever works for you, *do it!*

It may be necessary to depend on another behavior, such as exercise or going to support group meetings, to relieve tension or distract yourself. There is always the possibility that you will just trade one compulsivity for another. However, if you continually ask yourself if the steps you are taking are in a more positive direction, gradually you will be able to let go of all compulsivity. There will come a time when days pass without any fears associated with what you eat or look like. Remember, you are a worthwhile and important soul whose bulimia has served you in many ways. Be patient, be gentle, and let it go.

Can I take drugs to get better?

It might help, but even the strongest proponents of drug therapy do not recommend treatment based entirely on medication. Still, recent scientific data does support the use of MAO-inhibitors and antidepressants for the treatment of select patients with bulimia.

This is a controversial subject among clinicians. Most agree that individuals with eating disorders have mood disturbances, and many argue that bulimia is related to major affective disorder, the psychiatric family under which major depression is classified. There is also evidence suggesting that the cause of eating disorders might be traced to hereditary, genetic, and biological factors, including abnormalities of the hypothalamus, a gland in the brain which regulates many bodily functions.

A high percentage of bulimics have responded well to drug treatment and have lost the cravings to binge within weeks. These patients typically have a history of depression. In the past few years, fluoxetine (brand name Prozac) has been the most widely-used antidepressant, and many patients and therapists report good results from it as well as others. However, antidepressants do not work for everyone, nor will any kind of treatment. Draw your own conclusions by consulting with a professional trained in the pharmacological treatment of bulimia.

I do not have direct experience with drug treatment, although many people in our survey did. Close to 60% of those who had used antidepressants found them helpful in recovery. Several women indicated that drug therapy decreased their cravings to binge, allowing the issues that fueled the binge-purge behavior to surface.

Two of many psychiatrists I tried were biochemically oriented, and willing to modify pharmaceutical rules, based on their own experience. We kept trying different doses and medicines until something worked.

I started using Prozac, and it really helped me. My urge to binge lessened practically overnight. It made me feel more ready for therapy.

I am being treated with Parnate (an MAO inhibitor) which has changed my life. It offers a "normal" mood, as well as freedom from binges. Of course, therapy in conjunction with medication is the ideal situation, and I'm trying that too. I don't think one without the other would do.

How do I learn to eat correctly?

Just as there is no one road to recovery, there is no one way to eat correctly. Every individual body is different, and deciding what and how much to eat will ultimately be up to you. In the early stages of recovery, however, when emotions are high, food decisions are extremely difficult, sometimes immobilizing. It is helpful to have some plan with which you feel comfortable as you embark on new eating patterns. A qualified dietician or nutritionist, working in conjunction with your therapist, can help you with this.

As I indicated earlier, there are two main approaches to the food behaviors in recovery from bulimia. People who use the abstinence approach eliminate certain foods from their diet and stick to a food plan. This enables them to avoid those foods which might trigger fears about weight gain or binges, such as sweets, processed, or fried foods. One common practice is to have three, well-planned meals each day and up to three healthy snacks.

The other orientation encourages people to eat whatever food they want, in moderate portions, when they are physically hungry. This is certainly a more spontaneous approach and for this reason can be challenging, requiring a new awareness of hunger cues and permission to eat that which was previously considered "bad," without guilt. This approach can be easier with guided imagery or relaxation exercises before your meal, or eating with a friend.

Eating correctly obviously means not binge-eating or feeling badly about what you have eaten; however, it also means following a healthy, nutritious diet.

In our society, it is difficult for anyone to determine what foods really are healthy and which are not. Today's four food groups appear to be fast, frozen, fat, and fried—poor choices for anyone. Many restaurants serve overly large portions of fatty, sugary, processed food. With rare exceptions, fruits and vegetables are chemically treated, poultry and livestock are pumped with growth hormones, and much of our seafood swims in polluted waters. Finally, millions of dollars are spent promoting diet plans with powdery meal-substitutes or brand-name processed foods. Recovering bulimics have a particularly difficult time wading through this muck in order to learn how to eat nutritious meals.

A healthy, well-balanced diet includes complex carbohydrates, protein, fat, vitamins, and minerals. Carbohydrates are the body's primary energy source and are crucial to the functioning of the red blood cells, brain, and central nervous system. Therefore, it is important to eat whole grain breads, pasta, rice, and starchy vegetables, such as potatoes. Protein also provides energy, but if enough carbohydrates are eaten, protein is used to build and repair tissue and help maintain adequate immune system function. Animal products provide "complete" proteins, but grains and legumes (such as rice and beans) can be adequately combined within a 24 hour period to form "complementary" proteins, which are essential for vegetarian diets. The body also needs fat to provide and absorb fat-soluble vitamins, fatty acids, and to slow the emptying of food from the stomach, which gives a feeling of fullness. Good sources are seeds (such as sunflower seeds or corn) and unsaturated oils. A balanced diet with variety will provide the vitamins and minerals needed, although supplements may be appropriate. For more information, consult a professional or books on nutrition (not diet books).

Often, individuals with eating problems are well aware of these basic nutritional facts, but have difficulty acting upon them. This is because food represents much more than fuel. Changing your eating behavior may require trial and error in order to find a comfortable, healthy alternative to bulimia.

Eating normally means enjoying what I eat. It also means loving myself enough to nourish my body with healthy, adequate nutrition.

To normal eaters, food is just food; it's not a substitute for something missing in your life, or a way to stuff feelings.

There are no more "good" or "bad" foods. I eat when I'm physically hungry, and stop when I'm comfortably satisfied. I can eat the foods I enjoy whenever I am hungry for them, and I am more aware of the taste and texture. I no longer binge as a result of deprivation.

I no longer binge or purge, but I also have to watch how much I eat, and I abstain from certain foods such as wheat, flour, hard cheese, and crispy, salty things like potato chips or rice cakes.

Eating normally is being able to eat anything I want, in moderation, with anyone I want. Now, I enjoy going out to eat with my husband.

If I quit purging, will I gain weight?

There is no single answer to this question that is true for everyone. Some people gain weight when they stop purging, others lose or stay the same. This question is of obvious concern for most people with bulimia, but it brings up another, more relevant question: Why do you care? Whether you gain or lose weight is not as important as whether you can become self-accepting regardless of your weight or shape.

Currently, the message that thinness has innate value permeates every level of our society, although this has not always been the case. While there have been societal standards of beauty within every culture and time, emphasis has been increasingly placed on thinness in Westernized countries since the late 60s, particularly for women.

A thin body has become a panacea, with both implied and actual rewards. We asked people who have had food problems to list their gut reactions to the words "thin" and "fat." "Thin" was associated with goodness, power, success, glamor, comfort, control, happiness, approval, attraction, friendship, love, and perfection. "Fat" connoted the opposite: panic, anger, self-hate, inferiority, unworthiness, unhappiness, loneliness, frustration, disgust, desperation, laziness, rejection, lack of control, ugliness, sloppiness, and failure. As a culture we have been brainwashed. So much so, that we can no longer separate the uniqueness of a person from the meanings connoted by the size of their bodies. This creates prejudice, the ultimate result of which is discrimination against large people. Naturally, you are worried about gaining weight!

A diet proposes that a thin body is not only desirable, but it is universally attainable. For this reason, losing weight by dieting has erroneously become synonymous with self-improvement. No wonder we are overloaded with diet plans, diet books, diet foods, weight-loss centers, programs, spas, aerobics videos, exercise equipment, motivational tapes, and more! Ironically, many of today's models and starlets, while pitching everything from diet sodas to popcorn, are the same women who are also unhappily fighting with eating problems to stay thin and marketable. Face it, the diet craze has led to wealth for many people, and they all want to keep selling.

However, let's acknowledge a crucial fact regarding dieting and weight loss—DIETING DOES NOT WORK. At any given moment, some 20 million Americans are actively dieting, and 95% of them will regain that weight and probably more. Most of those people will blame themselves for this failure, but ultimately it is the premise of losing weight by dieting which is incorrect. The most basic reason why diets don't work is that the human body has a variety of survival mechanisms designed to maintain balance. These mechanisms perceive a restriction of food intake as an emergency, like starvation, and make adjustments so that the body holds onto precious pounds instead of letting them go. Let me explain.

According to "setpoint" theory, everyone has a genetically determined weight which is best for them—physically and emotionally. It is influenced by the foods we eat, the exercise we get, and the overall care we take of our bodies; but generally speaking, each of us has a natural weight our bodies "want to" be. This can be hard to accept, especially if we have looked for our ideal weights on standardized tables or in comparison to skinny models instead of within our own bodies. The fact is, though, that we can usually find our dress sizes on our family trees, and there is not much we can do about it!

The setpoint operates like an appetite and metabolic thermostat. If we undereat or skip meals, the metabolism slows down and burns fewer calories while our hunger increases. If we overeat, the metabolism speeds up, burns more calories, and our appetite drops. In this way, the body actually defends a particular weight range in an effort to maintain health and balance. So long as we are not starving or stuffing ourselves, we can eat a variety of foods—more on some days and less on others—and keep a relatively stable weight. Actually, there is not one ideal weight for each of us, but an ideal weight range, which is about five to ten percent of total body weight.

Furthermore, rapid water loss accounts for almost all of the weight decrease during the early stages of a low-calorie diet. When the body is deprived of blood sugar via restricted carbohydrate consumption, the liver will first break down its own stored sugar (glycogen), and then will convert amino acids from muscle protein into sugar. Both the glycogen and amino acid molecules are surrounded by water, which is then released from the cells, passes to the kidneys and is excreted as urine. For this reason, dieters can initially lose several pounds of water weight rather quickly. However, the kidneys adapt to this water loss by retaining sodium and consequently water. It is this adaptation that many dieters experience as a weight "plateau."

This water retaining principle combined with a decreased metabolism can cause a frightening weight rebound when the diet is over and old eating patterns are introduced. Even if a person continues to restrict calories, increasing their food intake over the diet level can cause large water weight gains. Also, that "loss of control" that occurs when dieters fail by bingeing is not due to psychological weakness. After experiencing starvation, the body sends out particularly loud hunger signals. Overeating is a natural consequence of deprivation. Animals in the wild do it, and humans do as well.

It is possible to lower our setpoint somewhat by increasing the amount of healthy aerobic exercise we get, choosing whole grains rather than refined carbohydrates, and decreasing fats and simple sugars. But restrictive dieting, purging, or any other method of trying to attain a weight that is significantly lower than this setpoint range will create physical hunger, tension, depression, anger, feelings of deprivation, and a preoccupation with food. In other words, your body is telling you it wants and needs more nourishment.

In answer to the original question, frightening though it may be, many bulimics who resume normal eating do gain weight. They must get their metabolisms back up to normal and replenish their cellular water supply. At the same time, though, they are making the commitment to gain happiness, peace of mind, feelings of wholeness and integrity, as well as take care of themselves emotionally and physically. Interestingly, many individuals from our survey discovered that when they gave up dieting and the need to be thin, their bodies came to rest at weights that were acceptable, comfortable, beautiful, and unique. They were not necessarily thin.

I'm content with myself and realize I don't have to be skinny any longer. My health is more important to me than the image of "model thin."

Nothing could hurt me as much as being called "fat." It's only now, with definite steps toward recovery, that I'm able to understand how I used food and weight problems to hide from the real issues: relationship problems, loneliness, and shyness. Only when I took recovery as serious business, was I able to understand that all of life does not revolve around fat or thin.

I used to weigh myself at least 25 times a day. Now, I have not been on a scale for over two years. Eating disordered people like myself are so hung up on numbers. What should count is how you feel, not a number on the scale. It's hard to break the scale habit, but my advice to anyone is don't weigh yourself at all!

My weight stays within a five-pound range. I will admit that I would like to weigh about five pounds less, but I consider stopping bulimia much more important than being "thin."

This increase (eight pounds) was right after I stopped vomiting every day, but I have stayed at that weight ever since.

I am at peace with my body image. I learned the way I look doesn't count half as much as how I act, and my attitude toward myself. I get more compliments on my appearance when I am feeling really good about myself than when I struggled to be thinner.

How should I choose a therapist?

Most bulimics should consider using professional therapy. I'm often asked for referrals for therapists, and at one lecture, I recommended a psychiatrist who was considered a national expert on eating disorders. From the back of the room, a woman immediately cried out, "Oh no, that man is horrible." She went on to describe her experiences with him, which were indeed terrible. Yet I know that he has helped others. It is important to find the therapist that is right for you. Would you buy a car without a test drive? I've seen people literally spend an hour trying to decide which ice cream to pick in a supermarket. Choosing a therapist should certainly take more consideration than that. Put in time and effort to find a therapist that will help you.

As I've mentioned, there are different approaches to recovery. You must decide for yourself which approach best suits your needs. When you investigate therapy options, consider whether you want to try the "abstinence" or "legalized" approach. However, be flexible and willing to re-evaluate your beliefs. Do what will work for you!

Local health agencies usually provide lists of doctors and counselors who treat bulimia, and hospitals and medical clinics often have specialties in this area. There are quite a few residential facilities devoted entirely to treating eating disorders. For some bulimics, hospitalization is an effective part of their treatment. (See the "Resources" section of this book.)

A "therapist" is usually a psychiatrist, psychologist, or marriage and family counselor, but there are other professionals who can also help, such as: licensed social workers, dieticians, registered nurses, clergymen, acupuncturists, or chiropractors. A multidisciplinary approach combines several professionals as a treatment team. If drug therapy is a consideration, a qualified physician must be part of that team.

Check in the phone book and make some calls asking for references. Referrals are a good place to start, but you have to kick their tires! Call their offices and ask for a short appointment to meet them. Let them know that you are also interviewing other therapists—they'll appreciate your effort. Come prepared with a list of questions. This will not be a therapy session, so your questions can be hypothetical or direct—it's up to you. Some things you might ask are: What is their treatment approach to bulimia? How often would you need to see them? How quickly might you see results? How long would they expect therapy to last? What will the charges be and do they have a sliding fee, based upon income and need? Do they accept your insurance?

In evaluating the interviews, use criteria that are meaningful to you. These are subjective measures. Probably the most important area to consider is how you felt during the interviews. If you were comfortable with the therapist and felt that you could honestly work with him or her, that's a good indication. Other things to notice: Do you like the office? Does the staff seem friendly? Does the therapist answer you directly or invite you to express yourself?

Finally, you can always change therapists. Once you've picked out someone, try a few sessions. Give therapy a chance. You might decide together on a reasonable time period before evaluating your progress. If therapy with your first choice proves unsatisfactory, find someone else!

I care about someone who is bulimic, what can I do to help?

If someone close to you has bulimia, face it together, but remember that they are the ones with the problem. Do not expect them to suddenly change unless they can come to this realization. Whether they are willing to quit or not, tell them that you love them and are available to help. The support of a spouse, parent, sibling, or friend is the most valuable tool they can have.

Keep in mind that bulimia is a protective device used to handle pain. Someone who uses food as a coping mechanism needs understanding and compassion. The reality of bulimia may shock or seem disgusting to you, but separate the individual from her binge-purge behavior. She deserves love and appreciation for who she is apart from the bulimia. If a loved-one became disabled or ill, you would still be there for them—bulimia is disabling and life-threatening.

Parents of bulimics need to be aware of limitations in helping their children. Loved-ones can research treatment options, read appropriate books, attend lectures, and talk to experts, but only the bulimic herself can do the work. Let her open up to you with her feelings, but if she does not make progress with your support alone, suggest recovery groups or professional therapy. Letting her know that you are willing to listen, and encouraging her to commit to overcoming bulimia, is as far as you can go.

At the same time, do not be manipulated or lied to for the sake of binges. Do not enable the disorder by looking the other way or pretending that the problem is not serious. If you stock the refrigerator with food only to have it flushed down the toilet, be honest and assertive about your rights and needs. Bulimics should not be allowed to abuse your trust or pocketbook; having bulimia is not justification for treating loved-ones poorly. Don't turn meals into battles—food is not the issue.

In many instances, parents have played a part in the cause of their child's behavior, and they may have to undergo some adjustments of their own. They may need to examine their own values and ways of communicating as well as trying to understand their child's problem. Guilt, anger, frustration, denial, and cynicism are all likely sentiments. You might also need to re-evaluate family rules about food, parenting roles, and the family's decision-making process. Being willing to honestly uncover and acknowledge the roots of her problems may mean facing issues of your own. Family therapy has proved to be one of the most successful methods of overcoming eating disorders. With patience, love, and increased self-knowledge, parents can better accept their own feelings and begin to help their child. (See the chapter, "Advice for Loved Ones.")

What can be done to prevent eating disorders?

In the past dozen years since I wrote the first publication in print about bulimia and began working to increase education about these matters, I've come across hundreds of books written on the subject, countless newspaper and magazine articles, television programs, movies, radio talk shows, and public lectures. Numerous eating disorders organizations and treatment facilities have come in and out of existence, there have been many enlightening conferences and workshops, and a whole new specialty has developed for health-care professionals. My efforts and those of other writers, speakers, organizers, therapists, administrators, and educators have helped real people. Also, due to increased public awareness, today's bulimics are able to find help more readily available and know that they are not alone with their problem.

Sadly, there are still thousands of individuals who suffer with eating disorders and countless others who are preoccupied with weight and body dissatisfaction. It is apparent that although we have defined bulimia and developed a variety of successful treatment programs for it and other eating problems, our long term goal must be to prevent these disorders altogether.

Healthy eating and the dangers of dieting must be incorporated into every elementary, junior high, and high school curriculum. We should further educate parents, prospective parents, teachers, fitness instructors, physical educators, clergy and others about the symptoms, causes, and consequences of eating disorders, with early detection and intervention in mind. Parenting classes, public forums, the media, and even casual conversations are avenues for learning and sharing this information.

Eating disorders education is only a stopgap measure however, because it is the underlying causes which must be eliminated. This is a lofty goal that would require a revolution of contemporary thought. In a perfect world, free from eating disorders, all people would appreciate that love and self-esteem are their birthright regardless of shape or weight. Families, aware of the causes and consequences of eating disorders, would be a constant source of communication and sharing. Women would be safe from victimization in their homes, in the work place, on public streets, and in the media. Inner beauty and competence would be recognized and rewarded without regards to age, color, or body shape. Food would a symbol of life rather than a tool for abuse. In other words, people would be allowed to be themselves without conforming to tight fitting roles based on artificial limits.

Obviously, we have a long way to go, but we must take any steps that lie in our paths. Striving for far-reaching goals means that each of us must first face prejudice in our own lives, and learn to embrace ourselves and others, regardless of differences. It is only within an atmosphere of mutual love and respect that we will fully realize eating disorders prevention on an individual, and ultimately a societal, level.

Lindsey Hall, age 3
(photo by LeMoyne Hall)

CHAPTER 2

Eat Without Fear
A True Story of the
Binge-Purge Syndrome

Introduction

I finished writing the story of my bulimia and recovery on my birthday in 1980. I printed 100 copies of the 32-page booklet which I titled, *Eat Without Fear*, and finally felt completely free from bulimia. Getting it all down on paper was the final purge for me! What's more, I felt that I had accomplished something which could help others because, at that time, there were no books solely about bulimia.

My bingeing and vomiting days may have been over, but my involvement with eating disorders education was just beginning. Those first 100 copies disappeared in a hurry, and I didn't give them all to my family! The booklet was reprinted 14 times, making apparent the need for information and education about bulimia and other food problems. In partnership with my husband, Leigh Cohn, who co-authored *Eat Without Fear*, I decided to continue to write and speak about the seriousness of eating disorders. We have been doing it ever since.

Beginning

I came from an affluent family that lived in a fancy home an hour north of New York City. My father commuted to the city, where he worked as an investment banker. My mother was active in environmental causes, country club tennis, and amateur photography. I had three older siblings who paid little attention to me—except for one sister who teased me unmercifully. I was seven when the fifth child was born, and my parents hired a live-in couple to take care of me and my baby brother.

The overall impression I have of my childhood is of being alone and afraid that I had done something wrong. I didn't mean to get in trouble; on the contrary, I always tried to be a perfect little girl. Nevertheless, I had the perception that I was constantly screwing up, like the time I put my sister's toy animals in a pillowcase to show to someone, not realizing they were delicate china and would all break. My father made me suffer for that mistake! One of my biggest goof-ups was accidentally locking myself in my mother's clothes closet. She went to New York, and I stayed there all day, crying and afraid. No one heard my screams, not the maid, the laundress, or my nanny. I was not found until my mother came home late that afternoon. Even though I was rescued, I felt like life in that house could go on without me and no one would notice. I was not the smartest, prettiest, oldest, youngest, or a boy, any of which I thought would have given me some importance in the household.

Most of the time, I retreated alone to my room, attic playroom, or the empty barns to play. I had a few friends who lived nearby, but I avoided going to their houses for fear of their parents. One of the mothers used to laugh or yell at me when I didn't want to eat. Another threatened to hit me with a wooden spoon, and I was made to sit at the table until I finished lunch. I was terrified of going there again—she made me eat tomatoes!

When I was ten, at an annual physical exam, I overheard the doctor tell my mother that I weighed too much. They said nothing to me, but after that I was conscious of my imperfect size. Salesgirls in the clothing store where my mother and I shopped for dancing-school dresses always sympathized with my "figure problem" and recommended "A-line" skirts. Despite my nickname at grammar school, "Thunder Thighs," I wasn't obese. By the age of thirteen, I weighed 135 pounds and was 5'5" tall.

I went away to a prestigious East Coast boarding school at age fourteen. Everyone else from my grammar school class went away to private schools, too, as the local public school was considered "lower class." Without realizing how afraid I was or how to communicate my apprehensions, I left home in tears. For months I cried at the slightest provocation. I had never approached my parents with problems and I had never confided in friends. I didn't even know what was bothering me. All I knew was that I was desperately unhappy.

The other girls at school all seemed beautiful and unapproachable: long fingernails, neat clothes, curly hair and THIN bodies. It was obvious that thin was "in" right from the start. I had heavy legs and thighs, which to me were the most disgusting forms of being "overweight." Being pear-shaped was an unspoken sin. I began to focus on my body as the source of my unhappiness. Every bite that went into my mouth was a naughty and selfish indulgence, and I became more and more disgusted with myself.

There were a few other girls whom I suspected had problems with food. One girl who roomed next to me for one quarter was always buying quarts of ice cream and hiding in her room. Then she would proudly announce that she was starting a diet which required fasting for the first two days. Another girl lost so much weight that her muscles could no longer hold up her 5'10" frame, and she walked bent over with her emaciated pelvis tucked forward for balance. She was taken out of school with anorexia nervosa, rumored to have been throwing up to get skinny. That rumor was the first knowledge I had of someone forcibly vomiting. Even the other girl who attended the school from my hometown pulled a "crazy" act by eating hardly anything but oranges for several months. I visited her in the infirmary where she had been sent for blood sugar tests because her weight was so low, and I didn't know what to say. I secretly envied her willpower and her protruding ribs.

By the time I reached my senior year, my crying in public stopped, and I was no longer outwardly unhappy. I played sports, sang in the choir, and had one good friend. She knew I thought of myself as ugly, and often reassured me that I was very pretty, but I honestly thought she was humoring me like my parents did. I avoided situations which would make me feel like a failure. I begged to be let out of honors math, refused to be nominated for any offices, rarely went to dances, and was afraid to talk in class. I was happy to get menstrual cramps once a month and retreat to the safety of the infirmary. I didn't seek out friends, and instead spent a lot of time alone or taking care of animals in the biology lab. I hoarded food in the dorm refrigerator and sometimes hid in my closet during dinner hour, sneaking food from my private stash. I kept a five-pound can of peanut butter from which I snuck teaspoonsful when no one was around. Thoughts of food were often with me although I had not yet binged and purged.

I often tried on clothes in front of a full-length mirror to see if they had gotten looser or tighter. I took up smoking cigarettes in private, which in my mind was a bad thing to do, but it was better than eating. I chewed gum, sometimes up to five packs a day. Through all this, I managed to hold my weight steady.

Then a friend went to a doctor who gave her a diet, and she lost ten pounds in one week. Playing down my desperation, I got my mother to take me to him. He gave me a pamphlet outlining the diet, and I returned to boarding school in the spring of my senior year thinking that my life was really going to change. I was going to lose the extra twenty pounds that sat between me and happiness; but the diet was horrible. I was weak and nauseous immediately. I was supposed to drink two tablespoonsful of vegetable oil before breakfast and dinner, eat only high protein foods, and drink 64 ounces of water daily. I lost eight pounds in one week, but felt bloated and nervous. Weak and sick, I went off the diet. I was a failure. At that time I had a boyfriend; but when the diet failed, I quit seeing him. I also had the word "change" in two-foot letters cut out and pasted on one wall of my room, but I no longer expected that to happen.

I started snooping in other girls' rooms to look at their belongings. Kept on a small clothing allowance, I could not afford anything but essentials. I sometimes "stole" clothes, hoarding them for a few days or weeks until the newness wore off, and then I would try to return them, unnoticed. Often an item was reported lost and there was a big to-do about how low a person the thief must be, and I would have to maneuver the circumstances so it looked as if the victim had just misplaced the missing item. I didn't want to be thought of as a thief; I just wanted to be like everyone else for a short time.

The most devastating thoughts, though, were that other people could eat and I couldn't. I would watch the skinniest, most gorgeous girl spread brown sugar and butter on her toast every morning and never get fat, never even seem to feel guilty! I was jealous of everyone who was thinner.

The first time I thought of sticking my fingers down my throat was during the last week of school, after I saw a girl come out of the bathroom with her face all red and her eyes puffy. She had always talked about her weight and how she should be dieting even though her body was really shapely. I knew instantly what she had just done. I graduated knowing that throwing up could be the solution to my weight problem.

I tried it three weeks later in a "Wimpyburger" stand in Oslo, Norway. I remember the secrecy, the pain of trying, and the excitement that I had indeed found an answer to my prayers. I *could* be thin. I spent that summer living with a Swedish farming family as an exchange student. They were a loving family, but I was unable to speak their language, and felt isolated and unsure of myself. I was afraid to decline food at any of their five daily meals! I tried to throw up at least once a day, but I couldn't always get the food to come back up. I was still experimenting. My weight got higher and higher, and I returned to the States weighing 175 pounds.

I shocked everyone—including myself—by being accepted to Stanford University, 3,000 miles from home, and I left in a blatant show of independence and bravery. Once alone in my dorm room, however, I was faced with loneliness and the hateful relationship I had with my Self. I retreated into eating to numb my anxiety, and I perfected the act of throwing up.

I began with breakfasts, which were served buffet-style on the main floor of the dorm. I learned which foods would come up easily. When I woke in the morning, I often stuffed myself for half an hour and threw up before class. There were four stalls in the dorm bathroom, and I had to make sure no one caught me in the process. If it was too busy, I knew which restrooms on the way to class were likely to be empty. Sometimes one meal did not satisfy the cravings, and I began to buy extra food. I always assumed that "this binge will be the last" and that I would magically and with ease metamorphose into a normal human being as soon as I threw up "this last time." I could eat a whole bag of cookies, half a dozen candy bars, and a quart of milk *on top of* a huge meal. Once a binge was under way, I did not stop until my stomach looked pregnant and I felt like I could not swallow one more time.

That year was the first of my nine years of obsessive eating and throwing up. I didn't want to tell anyone what I was doing, and I didn't try to stop. I was more attached to being numb than I was to anything else, and, although falling in and out of love or other distractions occasionally lessened the cravings, I always returned to the food.

I was convinced that bingeing was just a way to diet. There was nothing wrong with releasing tension by vomiting, even if I did it every day, and I consumed tremendous quantities first. I did not consider myself addicted, and I could stop anytime— probably tomorrow.

My letters home fluctuated between questioning why I was at college and vague complaints about my health. Letter after letter said the same things: "I'm afraid, but don't worry about me." "I'm sick, but I'm being brave and getting better." "I'm probably going through some phase." Usually there was a tidbit of news at the end. With every plea for attention, there was quick reassurance that I didn't need it; and, as much as I wanted them to ask me about how alone I felt, I would have denied those feelings. I know it. I was a smart girl, had been to the best boarding school, came from a family of lawyers, bankers, and Ph.D.s. I was very athletic, seemingly independent and "together." How could I admit that I was throwing up my food to be thin?

Living with a Habit

I moved off campus in my second year because I couldn't stand the pressure of being around people all the time. I thought it looked like the kind of thing a liberated female would do, and no one questioned the move. I arranged my life to accommodate my habit, pretending to everyone, including myself, that I was being more of an adult. I vowed that when I got to the new place I would stop the eating and vomiting because I wouldn't have people around to make me nervous. I'd start an exercise program, become infused with willpower, get thin, and the world would be mine. The only hitch was that as soon as I was alone, the bingeing and throwing up took over.

I decided what I really needed was a specific weight goal. I chose 110 pounds because I thought I'd probably look like a model at that weight. This goal stayed with me as an eight-year obsession, and I only reached it for one day when I was dehydrated from vomiting. Even then it made no difference in my view of myself; I thought I looked the same—fat!

If I bicycled home from school, I usually carried cookies and doughnuts to eat as I pedaled. Sometimes I got home and threw up that batch only to be overwhelmed with tension an hour later, and I would set off again for an uphill ride to the grocery store. Then I could glide home downhill, cramming cookies in my mouth after the frantic, desperate ride up.

I always bought the same foods: one package of English muffins, a pound of real butter, usually a package of frozen doughnuts, a bag of Vienna finger cookies, and always milk (preferably chocolate) or ice cream—and maybe five or six candy bars to start off the binge. I would even eat waiting in line. I told the checkers I was buying for a nursery school so they wouldn't suspect it was all for me. I could eat that much food in about an hour. If there was anything that I just couldn't finish, I threw it away, convinced and promising that this was the last time. If I hadn't bought enough food at the store, or if I was unable to get to the store at all, I would eat anything: a couple of omelettes or a batch of sugar cookie dough, a loaf of toast, or a whole cake. It didn't matter.

It was different now that I was living alone. There was no worrying if the bathroom would be empty or if anyone would think it strange that I came into my room with a grocery bag full of the same foods every day. The addiction was in control.

One imagined problem—not having enough money— became a reality. My parents sent me tuition and a small allowance, and I was in a work/study program testing mentally retarded children. I was happy about the work because it felt good to help others and it kept me away from food for a few hours at a time, but I always spent as much money as I earned.

It was at this point that I started stealing food. I felt a tremendous rush of independence and success when I got away with a bag of cookies or pound of butter. It was similar to my stealing at boarding school. I wanted what wasn't mine and what I felt was denied me. But there was one major difference, I did not plan on returning the goods. About six months later I was caught in a supermarket with a pint of substitute sugar in my purse, and the manager threatened me with jail. I promised to "go straight" and did, but the binges continued full force.

Marriage and a Secret Life

I had many short relationships that year which gave me attention, companionship, sex, and fun, but not what I thought was love. Then Doug, who was a friend of a friend, began to visit me and I liked being with him. As we spent more time together, I could tell that he was truly a good person. Ashamed, I decided not to tell him about my eating habits because I was sure that they would be changing "tomorrow" anyway. I was twenty and it felt nice to be in love. Due to his in-state military obligation, our two-year courtship was spent apart much of the time. When we were together for intense weekends, I would be free from the food obsessions. As soon as I graduated from college and Doug was finished with his military service, we moved in together.

We opted to look for jobs on the East Coast and stayed in an apartment over my parents' garage. My parents loved Doug even though we were unmarried and sleeping together under their roof, which made me feel that I had made a good choice.

The more he was included by my family, the more I retreated. Used to feeling unnoticed, I assumed that I was, and filled that emotional hole with food. I felt like an outsider, sneaking my sandwiches and cookies, and throwing up in a bathroom with a fan so loud that no one could hear what I was doing. Doug and I couldn't find jobs, and after six months, we moved back to California where he was accepted to graduate school. We also decided to get married. I didn't think it would matter that my mind was often elsewhere, dreaming about food, because on the surface I felt loved and in love.

Daily Life

For the five years I was married to Doug, the daily rituals and idiosyncrasies of my food problems became more and more rigid. I learned to put face powder on my eyes to hide the redness from the pressure of being upside down, and on my knuckles where they got raw from rubbing against my teeth. I routinely ran water in the sink to drown out the sounds of throwing up. I got on the scale every time I passed the bathroom, as well as before and after every binge. I methodically tried on my clothes in front of a full-length mirror, hoping they would hang looser than the time before. I became a meticulous housekeeper, especially when I did not have a job and was "working" at home. Sometimes I delayed throwing up while I vacuumed and washed dishes, eating all the time, to set the stage for the "cleaning" of my body.

I was averaging three to five binges every day, which necessitated covering my tracks. Between binges, I ran to the store to restock the food. I washed dishes constantly, and I was careful to clean the toilet to be sure I'd left no traces. I hoarded bulk foods. There were days when I had to rebake batches of brownies a couple of times. I wanted everything to be orderly and clean. *The only thing that was not just perfect was me!*

I was nervous in restaurants although we ate out a lot. For nine years I never ordered an entree because I was afraid I'd lose control. Instead, I ordered a few side dishes, but I'd suggest we get ice cream after dinner to polish off the secret binge. I always ordered whole milk, because it was thick and smooth and made the food come up easier. I even knew which restaurants had private bathrooms.

I read books on nutrition and health, thinking they would be a positive influence. To others I seemed like a health food freak. I took a course in anatomy and physiology because I thought that if I could see what I was doing to myself physically, maybe I would stop bingeing. I was always outside myself, separate from my behavior, wanting to control it.

I was surprisingly productive in those five years. I finished my B.A. from Stanford University, held two challenging jobs, and did creative projects on my own. I started a business which is still running, and I maintained relationships with family and friends, albeit from a distance.

After nine years of bingeing, however, I began to have physical side-effects which worried me. My vision often became blurry and I had intense headaches. What used to be passing dizziness and weakness, after a few of my binges had become walking into doorjambs and exhaustion. My complexion was poor and I was often constipated. I was usually dehydrated but didn't like to drink water because it made me feel bloated. Large blood blisters appeared in the back of my mouth from my fingernails. My teeth were a mess. Still, I refused to see that I had a serious problem even though the signs were obvious: poor health, an increasingly distant marriage, isolation, low self-esteem, fits of depression, and secrets.

Shift in Focus

In spite of the intensity of my addiction, and that I kept it all secret, Doug and I did have many happy and loving times. We never openly questioned being together, but he was committed to many outside activities, and I had food. When Doug got an offer for a fellowship at Cornell University, we moved back to the East Coast. I was unable to find a job there, so I decided to experiment with a batik process I had learned.

For a year I crammed my artwork between binges. I had two private showings of my designs, which gave me enough positive reinforcement to continue. At the end of that year, I decided to take my batiks, and some soft-sculpture dolls I had made, to New York City for professional feedback. I planned to stay with relatives whom I didn't know very well, which made me a little nervous, and I made appointments with designers. I tried to have confidence in my work and accept criticism willingly, but the pressure was tremendous. Several times, I stopped at a market to pick up huge stashes of food that I devoured in my room after everyone had gone to bed. One night, preoccupied by a binge, I left my papers where I had stopped for pizza and ice cream. I ran back through dark, unfamiliar New York City streets, oblivious to the danger. My food obsession had robbed me of rational thinking!

It was on this trip that I happened upon a magazine article about people who had problems similar to mine. The article was one of the first ever written about the bingeing and vomiting cycle, and the author considered "bulimarexia" related to anorexia nervosa, an illness characterized by self-starvation, but different because of the regular repetition of binges and purges. I was shocked! What's more, the author was conducting therapy groups five miles from where Doug and I lived!

My world suddenly shifted focus. I could not get the article out of my mind. When I returned home I spent a week bingeing heavily and then called the author, who told me to come right over. On my way, I stopped to stick my finger down my throat for what I was afraid would be the last time. What if she cured me today? I wasn't ready!

During the interview, I downplayed my lack of control and the severity of the problem. This was the first time I had told anyone! I don't know if the therapist guessed that I was holding back, but she invited me to join one of her ongoing therapy groups which would be meeting several days later. I told Doug that I had decided to deal with an old problem in a new way and added no details except that I was going for outside help. I stayed at home worrying that I would have to talk to a whole group of people about my binges.

When I got there, I presented my usual false front of confidence, because I was scared to admit that I was an addict. I didn't want to say exactly how many binges a day I did, how much food I ate, how much time it took, or how alone I was most of the time—but I did. To say out loud, "I throw up five times a day," was extremely hard. The women in the group were very responsive and supportive even though each of them was struggling with her own food issues. All along I had thought that I was the only person compulsively eating and vomiting, but the group helped me see that I was not alone. The therapist stressed the importance of taking actions such as speaking up, honestly acknowledging feelings, and keeping a journal. Sometimes I was able to put off binges for a day or two and I began to gain confidence that I would continue to get better.

I attended five sessions, then Doug transferred back to Stanford. Recovering from bulimia was becoming my focus now, but I was still afraid to tell him anything. Under the strain of my secret life and his dedication to his graduate studies, our marriage turned into a distant companionship. I decided that it would be a good idea for me to live alone for a while to concentrate on my cure. I told Doug that I would come to California too, but that I wanted my own place. I felt that we couldn't be together until *I had changed.* This was my addiction and I would return to him clean, pure, free, and independent when it was all behind me. He need never know.

When we got to California, we took separate places to live, which was painful and confusing for us both. We had never expected to be apart. Doug took an apartment in town, and I took a room in a house in the country. We saw each other daily, but it was always awkward. No matter what changes I felt inside, when we were together, I couldn't share them with him.

I liked Susan, the woman who owned the house where I lived, and I hoped that I could open up to her. But my bingeing began almost immediately, and I missed my group back in New York. I tried to keep up with my journal but was disgusted by my eating and wrote only about my daily life, not my feelings. Being around Stanford brought back many memories, and I returned to the same markets and doughnut shops that I used to frequent. Even though I had taken some daring steps towards curing myself, I still clung to the magical promise of getting better "tomorrow."

An art fair in Los Angeles was coming up in two months and I planned on selling my soft sculpture and batiks. I was hoping that it would be financially successful because my binges were expensive and I was running out of money. I kept on overeating and vomiting, assuming that when the fair came, things would change. I would make some money, spend some happy time with Doug, who offered to drive me, get some sun, and relax. I let my work on myself slide. Once again, my priority was not my cure, and I binged heavily until the fair.

Turning Point

I hoped that the fair would be a turning point for me and it was, but not in a way I had expected. Monetarily it was a bust, and I sold practically nothing. By the end of the third day, I couldn't stand the thought of going back for the final day. I was a bundle of nerves and even broke down crying with Doug and his mother, with whom we were staying. I could not tell them that my greatest worries were about food, so they could not help me. I faced returning to the Bay Area to live alone, without a job, and unable to confide in anyone about the food problem that dominated my life.

It was not these aspects, though, that made the trip a turning point. It was meeting Leigh Cohn, a man who was also selling at the fair. I quickly felt close to him, and we spent hours talking when business was slow. I had never felt so comfortable with anyone, and our conversations cut right to the heart—so different from my other relationships. I was conscious of his presence the entire time and did not want to say good-bye. We exchanged letters and phone calls and made plans to see each other a week later. He had taken a year's leave of absence from teaching to write and travel. When he arrived at my door, the attraction was incredibly strong. For the next three weeks, we spent almost every day together in what felt like a perfect union. Much to everyone's amazement, including our own, Leigh left his house, which was for sale in Los Angeles, to live with me in my one room at Susan's.

Doug reacted with disbelief, and we had many confrontations right from the start. My parents had been upset by our separation, but they found it incomprehensible that I was living with a man I had known for only a month while still married. Even Susan disapproved. It seemed like everyone was against us, and I didn't blame them!

Still, I felt on a very deep level that for once I was doing the right thing, and my Self blossomed in spite of the pressures. Unbelievably, the bulimia disappeared for several weeks. Leigh and I were together almost constantly and the sudden difference in my daily routine felt wonderfully healthy and refreshing. This seemed to be that magical, instantaneous cure I had always wanted.

As the days started to follow a routine, however, my new-found strength began to fail me. I worried about the hurt I was causing my parents and Doug. I felt guilty for being so selfish. I began to question if I really was doing the right thing and if I knew my own mind. After all, I ate and vomited for nine years knowing full well I was doing something crazy; maybe I was still crazy!

As my tension increased, I began to sneak food while Leigh slept and when I was alone working at my studio. I could feel the desperation and loneliness building as it had in the past, and I was frustrated that being so in love hadn't completely cured me. I realized that I had a lot of work ahead if I was ever going to overcome my bulimia, and that if I didn't take the initiative then, I risked slipping permanently back into the addiction. I wanted all of my life to be as wonderful, loving, and free of bulimia as those first weeks with Leigh had been. I finally decided to take a chance and tell him—otherwise there was only secrecy and hiding. This time I wanted honesty and love.

Ending the Behavior

In a tearful, emotional outburst, I told Leigh about my bingeing and vomiting. At first he didn't think it was a serious problem— "bulimia" was unheard of then. He had been a sweet-freak all his life, able to eat huge amounts of doughnuts and cookie dough without feeling guilty, gaining weight, or even getting cavities! He assumed that I was just a sweet-freak, too, and threw up because I felt guilty about it. As I described the size and the frequency of my binges, however, he could tell how desperate I was. He listened compassionately and resolved to help me.

I had always expected to get better *tomorrow*, but this time I knew that I had to start taking definite steps *now*. I made two resolutions. I would be absolutely honest and tell Leigh about all binges, and I would do anything to cure myself—even be locked away in a sanitarium if necessary. (At that time there were no treatment facilities specifically for eating disorders.) Leigh promised to stick by me as long as I stayed committed to my cure. He helped me come up with ideas about what actions I could take, listened, supported, laughed, and loved me; but we understood that it was my responsibility to stop the bingeing.

I went to see a psychiatrist primarily because of the tension and guilt I felt living with Leigh while still married to Doug. I didn't mention my bulimia at first, but when I did tell him, he recommended that I see a woman psychiatrist who had treated anorexics. I saw her once, but we did not relate well. I realized the importance of confiding in someone, however, and decided to continue getting support from Leigh.

There were several new activities that I wanted to incorporate into my daily life. I didn't do all of these things every day, but I tried to be as consistent as possible. I began meditating regularly and started writing in my journal again. I tried to establish a positive frame of mind and feel more relaxed. I decided to drink a certain amount of water each day, but I had a hard time with that, so I revised my expectations rather than feel like a failure. I also made lists; immediate goals, future goals, what to do when alone instead of bingeing, "Poor-Lindsey and Lucky-Lindsey" lists, what I liked and disliked about myself, how I felt about my parents, etc. I prepared a checklist of things I could do if I was on the verge of a binge, like exercising, sewing, gardening, taking a walk, soaking in a hot bath, and talking to Leigh or another friend about my feelings. It was often a struggle, but most of the time I fought the urge to binge.

I had to approach food in a new way. Rather than labeling foods as "good" or "bad" which gave them power over me, I wanted to learn to eat anything without fear. Toward that goal, I decided to allow myself one "forbidden" treat daily without guilt. This was a completely different orientation for me and was surprisingly easy. One major step I took was to go on a planned, all-day binge without vomiting. This requires a special preface. Although this activity had a tremendous impact on my confidence, to do it alone would have invited failure. *No one recovering from bulimia should attempt something like this without support and supervision.* On the big day, Leigh and I woke up to a bag of malted milk balls on the bedside table to start the binge *right!* We bought a pound of candy, a dozen doughnuts, caramel apples, caramel corn, a batch of homemade cookies, brownies, and drinks—all to take with us in the car on a business trip to San Francisco. During the course of the day we also ate hamburgers and fries, milkshakes, a greasy meal of fish and chips, and a continuous snack of white chocolate. By bedtime, we were both exhausted and stuffed. Leigh felt sick, but I was preoccupied by how my body looked and felt—pregnant and unable to lie down comfortably in any position. Leigh would not let me out of his sight for obvious reasons. I would never have tried this without a support person; undoubtedly, I would have vomited. In spite of my stomach cramps, I was actually quite proud of myself. I laughed at this incredible stunt I had accomplished.

The next day we fasted, which was almost as frightening to me as it had been to binge the entire day before. But, after keeping in so much "junk food," I wanted my system to rest. Fasting turned out not to be as difficult as I had feared and I got hungry again by evening. I was sure I had gained weight, but I hadn't, and that made me even more confident. This was a real turning point for me—I knew I could reach a goal, and I had power over food.

I began reading books that I thought might help me learn more about my inner self. I learned specific exercises I could do that enabled me to see how my values and beliefs were influenced by my parents and childhood. I also read books about spiritual masters whose lives inspired me to be more loving towards myself and others.

The most difficult thing that I had to do was to tell people the truth all the time. I started by sharing my bulimia with the people I least wanted to. Doug, who had finally accepted our separation as permanent, was astounded, but he took my confiding as a genuine act of caring. He said he didn't know why he hadn't asked me about spending so much time in the bathroom, and he was saddened by what I had gone through. I think we were closer after that than we had been in years.

About a month later, I substituted letter writing for journal entries. I always left open the option of not sending them or sending a revised copy. I wrote my parents letters about my recovery, but did not ask for or expect much participation from them. I began to confide in friends. Most were interested, sympathetic, and supportive, though a few dropped out of my life. I wrote the following in a letter to my childhood friend, the one who had eaten all those oranges at boarding school: "Finally, I can tell people about eating and throwing up. Do you know how ashamed I have been all these years, thinking I was abnormal and disgusting?"

I had a lot of pent-up energy that I needed to release in ways other than bingeing. Leigh and I wrestled on a large foam mattress on the floor and had exhausting fights with foam bats. I punched a boxing bag we had in our garage, and took long saunas. When I needed to, I screamed into a pillow until I was hoarse. All these things had a settling effect on my mind as well as my body.

During these months, I grew more comfortable with just being myself. I had always been desperate to maintain an image of unfailing perfection and independence, but now I stopped hiding my shyness, my anger, and my fears. Finally, as I grew to understand who I was and why, I also understood how well the bulimia had served me. It had been my friend, my buffer, my security, and my expression when I knew no other. As an addiction, however, it allowed no other behavior but itself and had taken me over. I fought hard to get me back!

The binges gradually diminished in number and size. During the first few months, I did several, but they dwindled to one every couple of months. When I did occasional binges, I tried not to consider them setbacks. I gradually accepted that a single binge did not return me to square one. Instead, I used those binges to better understand why I relapsed and what I could do the next time to intervene. With this understanding, the episodes became less and less frequent until they stopped altogether. It has been more than twelve years since I quit, and it has been many years since I've even thought about bingeing or purging.

The Healing Process

Ending the binge-purge behavior was only one part of my recovery, because the bulimia had touched every aspect of my life. Gradually, I have undergone a transformation in the way I view and experience everything, from a little conversation to a pressing crisis.

The most obvious change is in my relationship to food. I no longer eat to escape, nor am I obsessed about my weight or diet. I recognize hunger signals and eat accordingly. There are no foods I avoid, and I enjoy everything from nutritious meals to decadent desserts. I am perfectly capable of stopping when I am full, and feel no qualms about having seconds or leaving food on my plate. I do not follow any rules and have given up all of my compulsive rituals. I take good care of my body and generally practice healthy standards. I do, indeed, eat without fear!

I came to realize that my eating disorder had less to do with food than it did with feelings. Instead of being numb all of the time, I now experience life in a completely different way. For the most part, my waking state is one of peace and personal trust, although I do get happy, nervous, proud, frustrated, satisfied, concerned, sad, etc! I do have feelings, but mostly I am immersed in a state of love.

Being free of bulimia has brought me in touch with an inner self I never knew existed. This realization had a lot to do with honesty and trust. Once I made the commitment to always be honest, I stopped worrying about what I thought others wanted, and was able to focus on my own needs. As I learned to trust myself to make the best decisions, I discovered an inner self that would always lead me in the right direction. I came to respect and honor that inner self, and allowed it expression, so that other people could recognize my sincerity, goodness, and love. Instead of feeling worthless or only seeing faults as I had before, I now think of myself as funny, competent, creative, compassionate, and positive, and I think other people see me these ways, as well.

To close and get on with the important task of guiding your recovery, here is a brief update of my current life. Leigh and I married shortly after my divorce from Doug, and we continue to be deeply in love with each other. Our sons, Neil and Charlie, are great kids whose high self-esteems and generally happy lives are a daily reminder of the importance of valuing children's individuality and contributions. I also have a good relationship with my parents and siblings. My soft sculpture dolls were a national rage in the late 70's and early 80's. All that sewing certainly helped me to get away from my bulimia! Although I occasionally make one-of-a-kind pieces, my concentration in that area ended with close to a half million creations sold.

I now write and speak on eating disorders, self-esteem, and recovery. Leigh and I have co-written books in this area, and our publishing company, Gürze Books, is best known for *The Eating Disorders Bookshelf Catalogue*, a mail order service for books on food and weight issues. I am also involved with Eating Disorders Awareness and Prevention, the non-profit association that annually sponsors Eating Disorders Awareness Week throughout the United States.

As I said, we originally printed 100 copies of my story in 1980. Prior to this revised edition, there are about 75,000 in print, in various forms. The response has been tremendous, and thousands of people have used the information that is in this book to understand and overcome bulimia. I hope it will help you.

PART TWO

Overcoming Bulimia

CHAPTER 3

Where to Start

The Decision to Stop

Bulimia will continue indefinitely, unless a decision is made to finally end it. I advocate choosing not to binge for many reasons: live a longer, healthier, more loving life, enjoy eating, have honest relationships, reach potentials of creativity, save money. The list is endless. It does not really matter what your reasons are, just that commitment be combined with action.

Rarely, and never without some struggle, is a cure instantaneous. It takes bravery to confront even life-threatening behavior if it is serving to protect us from sadness, anxiety, boredom, spiritual emptiness, fear, a traumatic past, and other painful feelings. To give up that protection is scary; we are alone with an uncertain future and little self-confidence. Several bulimics we surveyed pointed out that they were "experts" on nutrition, health, and psychology. They understood on an intellectual level that their compulsive eating was unhealthy, but still initially resisted making the commitment to change. Most bulimics just wait and wish for a cure that will magically transform them without any sacrifice or work. When that does not occur, they must ultimately make the decision to end the bulimia. Everyone's reason for making that decision is unique to their circumstances, as these experiences indicate:

I've spent the last six months accumulating information on stopping bulimic behavior. However, I've avoided doing anything concrete. I've been waiting for that magic day when the bingeing would stop—each binge would be my last. Now hesitantly, shakily, I'm making a start.

Realizing that I am the only person who could stop my behavior helped me start my cure. It was all up to me.

Seventeen years is a long time to be in prison. I've done my time. I've earned my freedom. For me there are no concrete events or even attitudes in my cure, rather an existential decision in favor of life which I continually affirm.

Really, it was the decision to stop that did it. Then, I had to be quite forgiving to myself and give up my need to be perfect. As I began to eat better, I started eating less crap and craving less junk. It took me two years to stop craving food.

What has helped in my cure is seeking that cure. I became willing to try anything to find the combination of things that worked for me.

Several bulimics mentioned that physical complications caused them to question their behaviors. However, the mere knowledge of side-effects did not guarantee that a bulimic would stop. A bulimic nurse described her physical problems in quite specific medical terms, yet hid this information from doctors who were also her friends. A thirty-eight-year-old woman who spent thousands of dollars on dental work during fifteen years of vomiting felt fortunate that the damage to her body was not worse. Twenty-two percent of the bulimics that answered the survey were hospitalized for their symptoms, such as:

An experience that made a big difference to me was a near-death situation from poor physical health due to numerous daily bulimic episodes. I contracted malnutrition, double pneumonia, a spastic colon, and hypoglycemia. I was finally hospitalized for three weeks. Following my hospitalization, I got involved in an eight-week group therapy, which met four days a week for six hours daily!

Fear! My emergency hospitalization for cardiac problems due to low potassium was not premeditated or planned. Afterwards, I quit "overnight" and never went back to vomiting, but it was very difficult psychologically.

The dramatic changes in body weight and appearance which occur during pregnancy prompted several women to stop:

I had a premature baby who lived three weeks. My doctors said my bulimic behavior prior to the pregnancy had nothing to do with the premature delivery. I'm sure, though, that fourteen years of bulimia, in one form or another, had a great deal of impact on my body's ability to handle pregnancy. I thought this experience would be enough to "cure me forever," however, about three weeks after he died, I returned to old habits. I am again pregnant and I do not want to lose this baby, so now I am eating normally. I'm almost too strict with myself because I am so afraid.

My bulimic/anorexic behavior has ceased almost entirely because I'm pregnant. I feel so much love for this baby that I want to love myself, too. A deep caring feeling toward others can sometimes set you on the road to recovery.

The experience that made the biggest difference in my cure was becoming pregnant and giving birth. The role of my body took on a new perspective. The externally motivated desire to be thin—fitting into some societal prescription for beauty and happiness—was no longer in my reach. This gave me an opportunity to find or feel my own standards and to question "theirs" from my new, non-competitive, pregnant perspective.

Setting Reasonable Goals

One strategy that came up repeatedly was to work within a framework of success rather than failure. From this perspective, positive thoughts replaced negative ones, setback binges were opportunities to better understand the compulsion, and successes were rewarded with praise, happier feelings, and tangible results.

We received a survey response from one of the first women to read *Eat Without Fear*. She had been anorexic and then bulimic for twelve of her twenty-eight years. At first, she was relieved to read that someone else who was bulimic had "gotten well," and she went several days without bingeing. She then opened up to her husband, who was supportive, and she entered professional therapy. She now considers herself "cured" and wrote this quote about her early progress:

In the beginning, I had to make very deliberate decisions to do something else—to fight off an urge that I knew would only come back to haunt me again. I had to accept that each time I decided not to throw up was an experience that I could add to my repertoire of getting better. This allowed me to accept any failures because these failures never subtracted from my "getting better times." A failure did not mean all was lost. I could not throw up next time. I would use the failures to examine the circumstances that led me to throw up. From this I learned to avoid certain circumstances. At first, I thought this was weak, that I "should" be able to face anything to really be getting better. But I also had to face that I needed to build up my repertoire of holding in food so I could get stronger, and if that meant playing games with myself, that was okay. I became more self-accepting, which enabled me to feel better about myself. I began to carefully examine how I felt after I had thrown up and also how I felt when I didn't. I gained greater trust in myself and in my ability to get well.

Not a single survey indicated that a "cure" was immediate. In every case, recovery meant taking action, enduring pressures, and having some binges in the early stages. It also meant going beyond the bulimic behavior to understand the causes. Many shared that they tried to set reasonable goals, and some experimented with keeping simple contracts:

Basically, being willing to go through a whole hell of a lot of emotional pain and suffering has helped me the most. I make small, achievable goals, rather than overwhelming ones. Gradually, I have gone from seven times a day to once or maybe twice a week.

I plan my day and stick to the schedule, not allowing myself to "play it by ear" and panic at the first moment I feel alone, hungry, or unoccupied. It isn't regimented, it's guided. I set small goals and achieve them. I use a checklist.

I'm trying not to be obsessed with curing overnight. I know it takes time! Now I'm stopping after less and less food ingested than previous binges—two bagels instead of six. My therapist calls it "discreet amounts." My binges have lessened greatly. They used to be my whole day, my whole life. Self-love really helps and also not giving up. There's always tomorrow.

I used to give myself stars for every day I completed without throwing up. I bought the shiny colored ones like I got in grade school. For some reason, this worked.

I put $1.00 in a jar for each binge-free day and saved up for something I wanted.

Don't panic if nothing you've tried has worked yet. It's a battle you are fighting and it's hard to win each time. If you decide to stop the bulimic habit, you've got to expect occasional setbacks. Don't be too hard on yourself, but don't fool yourself either.

I stop myself from bingeing by recalling the pain experienced after bingeing; and, instead I do something positive for myself even when feeling depressed. Then I really "get into" feeling good about what I've done. This took me a long time to get to. I took baby steps the whole way!

Encouragement: Why Get Better?

The most important thing I can say about the struggle to end bulimia is that it is definitely worth it. Even though it is more of a journey than a goal, and it begins in what feels like total darkness, there is a light that exists within your own self, which will guide you on your path to health and wholeness.

Ironically, many individuals who have recovered from an eating disorder believe that they are better off in the long run for having had one and consider their problems with food and weight to have been their greatest teachers. Without it they might never have seriously questioned their beliefs and values or faced their inner fears. They learned to respond to old patterns in new ways, which enabled them to tackle other problems with confidence and compassion.

This might be difficult to fathom when you are overwhelmed by compulsion and self-loathing, but remember that eating disorders are not just about food and eating. They are symptoms of inner emptiness and pain which can be healed gently and gradually. In time, you will find other things which will fill you up not only physically, but emotionally and spiritually as well. As one person wrote, "Self-love can be delicious."

Inside of you is a creative, worthwhile, loving person. In your heart, you know this is true. Stick to your commitment, continue to do things instead of bingeing. Practice love, and believe in yourself. Make lists, get support, enter therapy, follow our two week program. It takes time for such a big change. Don't worry! Be willing to do anything to get better. You can do it! In the words of one woman who answered our survey, "My life has not changed with recovery, it has begun!"

Every aspect of my life has changed. I have tremendous value and self-worth. I am very productive, confident, enjoy beautiful relationships with family and friends, enjoy intimacy to the max, enjoy my children, am going through a divorce, and am happy about that, too!

Most of the time I'm fairly serene and better able to cope now that I'm no longer escaping through food. It's also more painful though, because I must deal with the emotions instead of covering them up.

Since I have been completely free of bulimia, I sleep better, have more energy, am less nervous, happier. I laugh more, and I'm told I'm more outgoing and fun to be with. I also have more money and more time to do the things I really enjoy.

I feel much more grown up, and that is wonderful. I am more confident. I don't avoid walking into a room of people. I approach each task with more strength. I enjoy little things. I am not so self-centered.

Physically I feel great. My hair is better. I just look and feel more attractive. I take better care of myself. I love my husband more. I am going back to college and I feel a lot happier and much more relaxed.

Suddenly, I have the time to get my work all done and play, too. I have much more money for hobbies. I'm settled now, happy, and eager for tomorrow.

It may sound terrible, but I was relieved when my bulimia was diagnosed. It called attention to my other personal problems. Had it not been diagnosed, I probably would have continued to have difficulties with relationships, depression, and self-esteem. I am proud of the person I have become, and it is only because I sought help willingly and stayed with it long enough.

Although the impact of my eating disorder has had many negative aspects, I feel that without it, I would not be the person I am today. I have had a reason or need to really discover my own truth.

I have ups and downs, like everyone else, but mostly my life is great! I feel happiness on a daily basis; I share love and humor and vulnerability with others. I never knew life could be this way, or that I could be this way. With recovery, I gained the self-confidence I never had.

I think I'm much more tolerant of others and their own difficulties than I would be otherwise. Also, I've become painfully and angrily aware of the ridiculous messages our culture passes on to young women. I literally fight it every day by offering opposing viewpoints to people who make shallow comments that seem to be accepted as the norm. I'm much more assertive than I used to be, and I feel more special and unique because of the growth in self-awareness that goes on in recovery.

CHAPTER 4

Get Support!

The struggle to overcome eating disorders is much easier with outside support. This can come from many different people, not only trained professionals. When bulimics say that I am the first person they told, I always encourage them to seek out a "next" person to tell. One college student enlisted the support of everyone on her dormitory floor. She made a public statement about her problem and asked that they all help her to stop bingeing. They responded in full force!

Most bulimics are afraid that their husbands, lovers, parents, roommates, or others will catch them bingeing or vomiting. They are embarrassed by the truth, and think that being face-down over a toilet is an accurate representation of their self-worth. Not only is the bulimia disgusting, but they believe they are disgusting for doing it.

Unfortunately, this self-loathing is the reason why many people are afraid to get support. Acknowledging the behavior to others means risking rejection, and if they have been hurt by someone close to them in the past, this risk may feel too big to take. Instead of allowing others into their lives, they develop resentments towards those people from whom they are hiding, withdrawing further into their obsession.

Being honest by giving up all of the secrecy and pretence can be frightening but a tremendous relief. Bingeing and purging takes a lot of energy and so does keeping it secret! It is important to remember that bulimia is not a reflection of the inner person, it is a tool used for protection. Unfortunately, it reinforces low self-esteem and creates a barrier to honest, loving relationships, as well.

Eighty-five percent of the bulimics surveyed acknowledged that secrecy was one of the most difficult obstacles to overcome, but their comments indicated the value of being truthful:

Coming out of the closet and talking to people has probably been most helpful.

A bulimic lifestyle is inundated with lies. Lying became so much a part of me, it was difficult to remember what was truth. I figured that if I told the truth and admitted my imperfection, I'd be in trouble. For me, breaking free meant always telling the truth and accepting myself like that—imperfect, but fully human.

I strongly urge telling the family and friends about bulimia. It's difficult to conquer alone.

Telling my husband after four years has helped me the most. He is supportive and I don't hate myself as much anymore because I'm not lying to him. Talking about it to family members and a therapist has helped a lot too.

Family Support

There's no denying that we are affected by our families, both genetically and socially. Even when we leave home, we bring attitudes and habits to our new environments. Whether you choose to include your family in your recovery or not, it is important to recognize how they have influenced you, and decide what to do about it.

Parents serve as examples for coping skills, attitudes, and eating habits, and set standards for ambition, perfection, and acceptance. Although they may not mean to confuse or be dishonest, their actions may send conflicting statements. For example, a child may be told not to eat before dinner, yet may see mother sneaking spoonfuls as she cooks. Or, facing his daughter's coming of age, a father might withdraw precisely when she needs him the most.

In order for your parent to be an effective support person for you, he or she must be willing to take a close look at their own attitudes and prejudice surrounding the same issues that you are facing—large bodies, women's roles, intimacy, spirituality, low self-esteem, effective communication, etc! They might not be bingeing and purging, but they share many of the same concerns that you do.

Parents have also established rules and myths for us. Some are direct, like: no dessert unless you eat everything on your plate, growing boys need to eat more than girls, or father always gets served first. Others are less obvious, like: emotions should be expressed by yelling, misbehavior is best disciplined authoritatively rather than with rational discussion, or boys can be trusted to stay out late but girls are less responsible and must come home early. These myths and rules may have served a purpose when they were created, but they do not necessarily apply to your present life.

Overall, 91% of the bulimics surveyed felt that their families contributed to their eating disorder either directly or indirectly. Some were able to turn to their families for support, but others said that their families could not relate to food problems, because they either ate "normally" or were also obsessed. Meals were often scenes of confrontation or hidden pain and resentment. Many used bulimia as a way of getting back at their families. In any case, the behavior was an added problem and in no way improved the relationships.

Family therapy coupled with assertiveness training can be extremely helpful, especially when the bulimic is living at home. In some cases, therapists require that the family be treated as a whole. This is because the methods of communication in eating disordered families are often ineffective and can be greatly improved by learning new skills. Ideally, this would be acknowledged by all family members, and improving their relationships would be a shared commitment. However, you might decide not to involve your family at all, because they may be too unapproachable, critical, or unwilling to attempt change. Sadly, some parents are unable to face their contribution to the bulimia. It is still helpful, though, to acknowledge their influence. (See the chapter "Advice for Loved-Ones.")

Here are some reflections:

Loved ones could not have helped me at all. I feel that my family was 95% of the cause. My mother and her entire family is obsessed with cooking, eating, and people's weights. The few times I have opened up to her, she has not been willing to understand, but just laughs the whole thing off and tells me I shouldn't worry about getting fat.

Moving away from my family helped, because I got away from their constant criticism and judging of me. My parents always made me feel as though I wasn't really my own person, but rather a reflection of themselves. All of the neighbors and relatives would surely be watching to see how I turned out. Mom and Dad's success or failure would be judged, so I had to be perfect.

My bulimia has decreased almost 90% and I have my parents to thank for that. They have been very supportive and are always there when I need help.

I have difficulty getting support from my family, especially admitting to them that I need the help and asking for it, since I have always been the one to help and support others.

The biggest help in my cure was the Sunday night reports I would give my mom. After an entire week without bingeing or purging I told my mom about my accomplishment. I could see the relieved expression on her face, and that was enough to get me through any rough spots I encountered through the week. As each week went by it became increasingly easier to not throw up. Whole days went by without even a thought of vomiting.

When I reached adolescence, my father seemed to avoid me, and I thought it was because of my weight. When I told my parents about my vomiting, he showed the love and concern that I was missing. Having him involved in my life helped me most of all.

I've been bulimic for twenty-two years and my family does not know. I am still afraid to tell them.

If you are a family member, do not coerce the bulimic into therapy with the belief that you are immune to counseling. You might play an active part in her history and recovery. Be ready to take a deep look at yourself and your own coping patterns.

There has been a vast improvement in how I regard my parents. Hatred is replaced by love and understanding on my part. A show of more genuine affection is now shown by them. All of us are more honest.

Professional Therapy

Most bulimics agree that talking about their food problems is extremely difficult, but a tremendous relief. Professional therapists are excellent choices for this kind of support, because that is their profession! While bulimics may be embarrassed to "tell all" to a friend or family member, especially at the beginning of recovery, a therapist has no investment in seeing them as "perfect."

One feeling that a few individuals expressed was that no one other than a bulimic could truly understand the pain. While this may be true, professional therapists are trained and paid to listen, empathize, and provide coping skills. They offer guidance, acceptance, and knowledge about self-discovery. They will fully "be there" for their client and this is crucial for overcoming those feelings of loneliness and disgust which tend to perpetuate bulimia. We strongly recommend that all bulimics seek out some form of professional therapy.

There are many kinds of therapists and therapy techniques used for treating eating disorders. It is important to find the "right" therapist as well as approach. Some women stated that they had seen five or six different therapists before finally finding one who helped them. Remember, "therapist" is a term which most often refers to psychiatrists, psychologists, or marriage and family counselors, but sometimes applies to licensed social workers, nutritionists, school counselors, clergymen, acupuncturists, hypnotists, chiropractors, and others. Some therapy formats are: individual sessions, group sessions specifically centered on bulimia, groups with various types of eating disorders or issues, family therapy, in- or out-patient treatment, and halfway houses. The lengths of treatment vary from a few sessions to several years. (See "How should I choose a therapist?" in Chapter 1.)

Professional therapy received the highest praise on the surveys. Eighty percent found it helpful, and it was rated "most help" much more often than any other category. These comments represent the feelings of many other bulimics who also wrote about therapy:

Locating the right therapist for me was the most important element. Involvement in a self-help group was valuable.

I saw many different therapists, from psychiatrists to non-credentialed counselors, but the last therapist I saw was the only one that helped me!

My therapist has helped me to look at many aspects of myself that I was either unconscious of, or that I had pushed aside because they were too painful for me to deal with.

Seeing my psychiatrist by myself and at times with my mom has been the best help to me.

I give my therapist a lot of credit. She never pushed me or put me down. She kept the attitude that I'd do it when I was ready.

The thing that has helped me the most is my group therapy. It enables me to see others with the same problem, and is the only place I feel I can be honest.

One of my teachers recommended I go to the counseling center at school. This was the best move I could have made. My counselor has been very helpful. She has helped me talk about feelings and anxieties which were being ignored or substituted for by my eating.

The most effective treatment which I have experienced was working with a team of a psychologist and a dietician. We began working on a goal-driven plan, adding a new goal each week. Through this plan, I progressed from purging every time I ate to keeping down up to sixteen meals!

Eating Disorders Treatment Centers

There are many hospitals and clinics that have special eating disorders treatment programs. Typically, these centers have both in-patient and out-patient services, and employ a mult-dimensional approach using a team of skilled professionals, including: a medical director who is often certified in psychiatry, a program director, a psychologist who specializes in eating disorders, licensed clinical social workers or marriage and family counselors, a registered dietician, plus a well-rounded medical and nursing staff. Treatment can include individual and group therapy sessions, nutritional counseling, assertiveness training, relaxation and exercise programs, experiential therapies, and sometimes the use of medications.

Regardless of where you live, there are probably treatment centers nearby. Also, many general hospitals have eating disorders units. Consult your local hospitals to see what programs they offer, and for more information see the "Resources" chapter.

Other Support

Support was found by the survey members in many kinds of relationships, ranging from close friends to support groups. A few women described the value they placed on the unconditional love of pets, ranging from horses to dogs to fish! Free help can usually be found by contacting local college health or counseling centers, which may have on-going support groups. Many hospitals and individual therapists also sponsor free or low-cost groups that are open to the public.

Another no-cost option that has worked for many people is Overeaters Anonymous. Most communities have OA chapters, and many have groups specifically for bulimics. Check your local telephone listings for meeting times and places. Their national headquarters is also listed along with other eating disorders organizations in the "Resources" chapter.

We stress that it is up to you to take action! There IS support if you look hard enough. We state this again and again, because it is so important, as these quotes indicate:

The biggest key I've found is expressing myself and reaching out to others for help. In talking with other bulimics and asking people to listen to me, I gain a sense of who I am, relief from anxiety and anger and a secure feeling that I am okay. Today I have over seven months of no vomiting, part of which I believe is a spiritual miracle, and part is my willingness to show others who I really am.

The fact that most people close to me were not repulsed by my behavior made a big difference.

I felt a lot less isolated after opening up and bearing my soul to two trusted girlfriends. Their prayers and undying support meant a lot. I learned that I was not unacceptable as a person, even if I did have an eating disorder I hated.

I had a friend call me every night and I would tell her how I did. Knowing I was going to talk to her helped me to make the decision earlier not to throw up.

I encourage group support. Many heads together give different insights to problems.

Talking to my friend, who was anorexic and bulimic for eight years and is recovered for three, is always helpful.

Any support group where people share their honest feelings is helpful. Isolation is the bulimic's greatest enemy.

I have done a dozen or more things that were attacks on my compulsive eating, and I can point to aspects of each that have been valuable to me: the nutritional information from Weight Watchers, the comraderie and spiritual focus of Overeaters Anonymous, the increased self-esteem and general living strategies from counseling and growth experiences, the surrender and letting go from spiritual awareness, and the continual support from someone close to me.

Although many women described difficulty opening up to their husbands or lovers, the response they received was usually very supportive and helpful. Most spouses do an excellent job! These examples are a small selection of many similar remarks:

The most important factor in my recovery has been the support of someone who loves me unconditionally, in spite of who I am and the ugliness of my problem. My husband now, boyfriend during many of the years of my bulimia, did not reject or leave me when he found out about my vomiting. He also never lectured me about giving it up. He did not, however, shield me from the truth of the physiological danger from my actions. In fact, he told me that I would most likely die from some direct or indirect effect of my bulimia if I did not give it up. The way he put it, though, made it clear that whether or not I did so, I would be doing it mostly for my own benefit—although clearly he would benefit, too. He told me later that he had thought over all the approaches he could have taken with me and came up with the only possible one he could. It required tremendous restraint at times, especially when he was filled with worry for me.

My lover helped me greatly by being very uncritical. Her feelings of love and acceptance took the pressure off. Telling her when I failed allowed me to deeply experience my sadness yet know I was still loved. She had faith in my ability to recover.

Medical and Dental Examinations

If you are bulimic, it is likely that you have done some harm to your body. For this reason, you should have a complete physical examination from a physician who is familiar with bulimia, and who will encourage you to care for your body.

The secretive nature of this addiction kept the medical profession in the dark for a long time. Fortunately, most doctors are now familiar with its symptoms and side-effects. Be sure yours is. If not, ask for a referral from a local treatment facility or therapist who specializes in eating disorders.

Sometimes doctors are intimidating because of their time constraints and implied stature. Be assertive. Do not make excuses to avoid a physical examination. The cost is no more than a few binges, and in most areas there are clinics available with sliding fees. Be sure to tell the doctor your complete bulimic history. It is important to be honest.

It is also important to have a dental check-up, especially if you vomit. Stomach acid removes tooth enamel, and constant exposure to food, especially sugar, causes serious tooth and gum decay.

My teeth were an absolute mess for years, and have cost me thousands of dollars worth of dental work, but I have not had a single cavity since I stopped bingeing.

I was afraid to go in for a check-up, but my therapist insisted. Finally, I went for an examination, terrified that I had every problem that I had read bulimics get. To my relief, I was okay, and that made me feel better about myself and my recovery.

I was a rock-bottom bulimic and was hospitalized with low potassium. The doctors couldn't believe I wasn't in a coma! As I lay in my bed hooked up to an IV, I decided that the bingeing and vomiting just wasn't worth it anymore.

I had to educate my family doctor about my bulimia.

My gynecologist found a benign tumor the size of a grapefruit attached to the base of my spine. She didn't say that it was caused by the bulimia, but I believe that it was.

CHAPTER 5

What Has Worked for Many

Recovering bulimics need to develop new, healthier habits as they explore unfamiliar and often scary territory. They are discovering not only the origins of their problems in the past, but are radically transforming their behaviors in the present. As uncomfortable as this feels at first, it's like starting any new venture—it becomes easier with time and rewarding on different levels. If you are starting to recover from bulimia, there are practical suggestions in this chapter. Many of these ideas come from individuals who answered our surveys, and therapists who specialize in this field. Think about each of them as they relate to you, and concentrate on those which you feel will help you the most.

Acceptance

There is a saying, "What you resist, persists." If you have an eating disorder, there is a strong possibility that you are resisting something in your life or within yourself which is manifesting itself through your behavior. It might be a hurt that happened a long time ago, a belief which causes you low self-esteem, feelings of powerlessness, or something about your present circumstances which upsets you. Whatever it is, resisting the memory, the reality, or the feeling of it, gives it life in some aspect of your bulimia.

Accepting the fact that there are underlying reasons for your bulimia does not condone it, nor should it diminish your motivation for change. Quite the opposite, understanding that you are using bulimia for a purpose can ease the guilt and self-loathing associated with the behaviors, and make clear the fact that you do have choices in the present no matter what has happened to you in the past. Being honest about the role that bulimia plays in your life is a way of getting to know yourself and ultimately to care for the inner person that you have hidden for so long.

I want to accept myself and not feel the compelling urge to be perfect as reflected by my old need to be perfectly slender.

At first, I thought if I threw up even one time that I was weak. I "should" be able to face anything to really be getting better. But I also had to face that I needed to build up my repertoire of holding in food so I could get stronger. I guess I had to become easier on me. In doing so, I became more self-accepting, which enabled me to feel better about myself.

A great decrease in my bulimic behavior occurred when I got a dog. The dog represented acceptance, companionship, something to love and care for, which was missing in my life. Gradually, I began to accept and care for myself, as well!

Express Yourself

An eating disorder is a way to say something that we are unable to say directly. For example, expressing anger by stuffing food and violent purging may be easier than confronting someone who has hurt us. In order to give up using bulimia as an emotional buffer, you must risk revealing who you are inside and what you believe in. You are different from other people—everyone is—and that's okay! Here are suggestions for how to begin.

Think about what you say and how you say it, to yourself and others. Try increasing your use of the pronoun "I," and follow it up with active verbs such as feel, think, want, wish, am! Say "do" instead of "don't!" Stop thinking of yourself as "bulimic," you're "recovering from bulimia." The mind can create problems or solutions, it just depends on what you practice. Try positive self-talk. Repeat phrases like, "I love myself," and "I am great!"

Instead of swallowing your emotions, let them out. See if you can determine what your bulimia is saying. Give it a voice. If you are angry, punch a boxing bag or scream out loud. If you need to confront someone and are not sure how to do it, rehearse beforehand with a sympathetic friend or even in front of a mirror. You might write out what you'd like to say. Consider role-playing the conversation. Abandon your fears about talking to people; be honest. Express your opinion! Seek out uplifting friends and express your support of each other. Let your family and friends get to know the *real* you.

I have gone from a person who went along with everything anyone else said or did, to someone who has and expresses opinions of her own and knows what she wants.

From the moment I first told my parents that I was "recovering" from bulimia, my whole perception about myself changed. I started to feel more in control of my own decisions.

I discovered and am actually pursuing my own dreams.

Journal Writing

Individuals with eating disorders not only find it difficult to discuss their private thoughts, but in many cases have a hard time even knowing what their thoughts and feelings actually are. A journal is a safe place to explore this inner life. Writing is a form of intimacy in that it necessitates an honest, caring relationship with yourself; and giving your innermost thoughts and feelings tangible form builds trust. A journal will also provide a record of patterns that might need to be challenged, and it can be used to chart your long-term progress. Consider a dream journal for all the same reasons. Buy a nice notebook and keep it in a special place. Treat your journal (ie. your own inner experience) with love and respect.

Be spontaneous and let the words flow. No one else will read what you write, you won't be graded on content or grammar, and you don't have to explain yourself. You can be honest without being afraid. Schedule a block of time every day for writing, and use your journal during times of stress as well as contemplation. If you do not have something to write about, try answering questions such as "What's wrong with big thighs, and who says so?" or "What happened just before my bulimia began?" Fully answer the questions, going off on tangents. Putting the thoughts down on paper (or into a tape player) will literally take them off your mind! (We've added more on journal writing, along with writing topics, in "A Two-Week Program to Stop Bingeing.")

I have kept detailed journals over the past 15 years. When I really want to remember how distraught and obsessed I was, I can always read these by the volume. I am reminded of how far I have come, and how my desire for life, love, and happiness keeps me strong and clear.

When I began my recovery, I tried to make the journal my friend instead of the bulimia. In it I said whatever I wanted to say, knowing that it wouldn't judge or reject me.

Putting my thoughts and feelings down on paper was like making them real. It made me feel less isolated — like I would eventually be able to communicate with people better.

Physical Exercise

Exercise is a wonderful way to enhance our feelings of well-being and general health, but there is a fine line between healthy moderate exercise and working out obsessively. For someone with an eating disorder, exercise can be a type of purge. While it is healthy to jog 10-12 miles per week, running 10 miles per day goes far beyond the scope of proper fitness.

Some researchers claim that chemical changes within the body cause an exercise "high" which is addictive. While this may be true, exercise, particularly punitive exercise, is also an effective way to: purge unwanted calories, seemingly regain the control that was lost during a binge, release overwhelming emotions, and pass the time. Worst of all, excessive exercise can masquerade as a fitness regime and trick us into thinking we are being good to ourselves when we most certainly are not.

On the other hand, *healthy* exercise can be a tool for recovery, as part of a multidimensional, self-nurturing program. It was considered helpful by more than 80% of the bulimics surveyed and was described as extremely satisfying, mentally, emotionally and physically—as long as it wasn't a purge. We do not suggest one form of exercise over another. Team sports or group activities are just as helpful as working out by yourself, and you may find that there is more to be gained by being with others. Walk with a friend! A twenty or thirty minute vigorous activity every other day is plenty.

We stress the importance of a positive attitude, stretching, and allowing yourself time to relax and reflect afterwards. Take advantage of all the good feelings that come from moving your body! (There is a short guide to stretching on Day One of "A Two-Week Program to Stop Bingeing.")

I've found exercise to be very helpful. Afterwards, I'll tend to eat normally instead of my usual cram session. I jog, but I suppose any type of exercise that works up a good honest sweat will do!

To help ease anxiety and frustration, I swim or bike ride. This releases a lot of built-up energy that I usually use for a binge (bingeing is exhausting!). After exercising I feel so much better about myself. I'm proud because I chose to do something good for me instead of the same old reliable binge.

I used to jog two miles a day, went to five, and then added a workout at the gym. Sometimes I hadn't eaten in a long time and felt dizzy and weak. When I started to recover, it was hard to normalize both patterns at the same time, so first I quit exercising altogether and just concentrated on my fear of food. After I was able to tolerate feeding myself fairly well, I added walking, and now swim or jog a few times a week. I'm really doing well.

Daily exercise is essential for my mental, emotional, physical, and spiritual health. I try to do some aerobics every day, walk, swim, bike, etc. But if I miss a day, that's okay too.

Exercise makes me feel good, look better, and sleep great. It helps me have more energy, makes me feel strong, and eases stress.

Relax, Relax, Relax!

People with eating disorders have unhealthy stress levels. Although the bulimia can be calming in its mindless repetition and emotional numbness, its effects do not last. In the long run, a food addiction adds stress. Relaxation has the opposite effect, allowing the body to return to its natural, balanced state instead of being in a fight or flight reaction. Vision, hearing, blood pressure, heart rate, breathing, and circulation return to normal, and one is more capable of handling emotional pressures.

When you do begin to relax, emotions might surface. Let those feelings exist without dwelling on them any more than the wide variety of thoughts that will pop in and out of your mind while you attempt to quiet it. After your relaxation session, cope with any of the "old stuff" that came up in new ways (ie. talk to a friend, write in your journal, etc.), which will enable you to stop using food as a drug.

Here are a few ways to relax. If you're always on the move, slow down. Watching a bowl of fish for twenty minutes each day reduces anxiety. You might benefit from listening to music, taking a bath or a quiet walk, staring at a body of water or a fire, bird-watching—anything which rests your mind. I enjoy meditation in particular, because not only do I relax and get time to myself, but I always feel loving when I am done! There are many books and tapes available which teach different relaxation techniques. A description of one simple way to meditate follows, and others are included in the programs later in this book.

Give yourself at least a fifteen or twenty minute slot of time. Comfortably sit or lie down in a peaceful spot. Gently close your eyes, and remind yourself that you are a good person, deserving of great love and respect. Silently count to ten as you inhale, again to ten as you hold your breath, and once more as you exhale. Repeat this three times to slow down and to focus your mind. Then repeat "I am," with each breath, and continue this until the time is passed. (You may substitute other words, prayers, or a mantra, for "I am," but it is helpful to maintain repetition.) Try not to be occupied by your thoughts, but allow them to pass through your mind, and bring your repetition back in focus. This takes practice, and there will be times when your mind will refuse to slow down, but eventually you will be able to enjoy a state of deep relaxation.

Spiritual Pursuits

Eating disorders are about feeling empty inside, not just physically or emotionally, but spiritually as well. They are tools for coping with a life which lacks love, meaning, a sense of safety, empowerment, and self-esteem. Exploring these areas is what I call spiritual pursuit.

The most fulfilling, nurturing, mysterious thing I have done throughout my recovery has been to practice love. This has been my path—loving myself and loving others. This simple teaching forced me to look at every single barrier I had to experiencing love in all areas of my life. I'm not talking solely about love for a mate, but a pervasive *state of love* with which I could approach every person, place, and situation. Being on this spiritual path has given my life meaning and satisfied me in a way food never did. Ironically, I have my eating disorder to thank for it!

The bulimics who mentioned spirituality as one of their therapies—42% of all the responses—described "Spiritual Pursuits" helpful. They usually were deeply inspired and motivated, regardless of their faith. Many specific religions and practices were mentioned, but the underlying message was that recoveries were aided by faith in God as defined by each individual. Many people practiced self-love and love for others with the same spiritual effect and positive consequences.

The main thing that has helped is my faith and trust in God. A lack of security is a problem with eating disorder sufferers and knowing God cares for me gives me comfort and peace. We all need someone to trust, whom we know loves us unconditionally, not for how we look or what we do, just for us as we are.

An eating disorder is just a symptom that something is seriously wrong in our lives. In fact, it is an invitation to grow, emotionally and spiritually. Every crisis is an opportunity.

Today, I am reclaiming my feelings and working very hard to see that I am lovable and valuable: I deserve to live a joyous, fulfilled, serene life. Many times I've gone walking instead of bingeing, and I've never come home still wanting to binge. Usually I pray while I walk, pouring out all of my burdens, fears, joys, and hopes, knowing that God is hearing me, and delighted in me. I really enjoy this time alone with Him.

Practicing self-love instead of self-pity is important. Having faith and confidence in myself also helps.

Recognizing Hungers

There are two types of hunger: physical and emotional. They are not the same, but people with eating disorders treat them the same way—they eat. Physical hunger is our body's physiological craving for nourishment. Emotional hunger is wanting or needing to express strong feelings and not being able to. It is also a craving for those things which are missing from our lives like change, love, creativity, or satisfying work. Bulimics respond to both kinds of hungers by eating until they can literally hold no more food, but all of the food in the world cannot satisfy emotional hungers. Therefore, an important aspect of recovery is learning to recognize the difference between physical and emotional hungers, and to feed both appropriately.

For someone who has been bulimic for a number of years, physical hunger signals are extremely difficult to recognize. Some recovering bulimics respond well to food plans, which remove the responsibility for choosing when and how much to eat. These can be particularly helpful in the early stages of recovery, when emotional hungers are surfacing. However, other individuals choose a more spontaneous approach, legalizing foods and easing restrictions in an attempt to experience their hunger cues as they naturally occur. Whatever approach you take, remember that your metabolism will need time to readjust when the bingeing and purging significantly lessens or stops.

I believe there are two separate hungers. I feel best about myself when I eat in response to physical hunger. This feels like I am honoring my inner self. To eat in response to emotional hunger, without the presence of the physical, is my definition of compulsive eating.

I used to binge when I was upset, bored, or anxious. Now, I think about my feelings, and try to find alternate things to do.

I am learning through self-awareness and therapy that I have often chosen to eat rather than feel anxiety and anger. I am now able to express my anger and sit with anxiety. I understand that feelings pass and that I can choose not to eat.

Being terribly abused by the man I loved was the precursor to my bulimia. I binged to stuff the hurt and fill the void. Now, I am filled with love, but it comes from within me, not from someone else.

Without realizing it, I substituted food for many emotions. In my recovery, I'm learning to recognize that my sudden hunger or cravings are actually emotions or signs of something bothering me.

Body Image

Sadly, being unhappy with your appearance is a socially acceptable position for women in our culture to take, as though it was part of the female condition! Our mothers, sisters and friends were dieting when we were young, and they are still dieting. New weight loss programs continue to appear and the media and advertisers still use thin, young models almost exclusively. We have been so bombarded with the message that thinner is better that it is almost a revolutionary thought that we could feel at home in our bodies!

The discontent goes deeper than the surface, however, because a woman's body image is closely aligned with her self image. In other words, how a woman feels about her body usually mirrors how she feels about herself. If she is self-accepting and self-nurturing, she will most likely accept and nurture her body, too. If she is overly perfectionistic and punitive towards her self, this will be reflected in her feelings towards her body. For this reason, no matter how good you feel about conforming to an external ideal, you won't like your outer self until you like your inner self. Other people can even tell you that you are beautiful, but unless you feel self love on the inside, it won't make you any happier with your body.

Let's start with a dose of reality—bodies come in all shapes and sizes and you have been born prone to a certain body type which you can find somewhere on your family tree. Shape can be altered to some degree by the food you eat and the amount of exercise you get, but obsessing about looks you inherited is fruitless. Also, be aware that phrases like, "I feel fat," and "I look ugly," are an indication that there is something bothering you that goes beyond the way you look. Finally, because people with eating disorders have a distorted sense of body image, you probably think you look heavier than you actually do.

Here are twenty quick ideas for improving your body image: Smile more, look happier. Walk and speak with dignity. Let your body language reflect this emerging pride. Go to a dance or yoga class and leave your inhibitions at home. Use affirmations to change negative self-talk. Try guided imagery and visualization techniques to support self-acceptance and to handle fears associated with body changes. Make friends with some large men or women. Practice movement exercises to reacquaint yourself with how your body feels. Appreciate your sexuality. Have an orgasm! Take a couple of days off for a personal vacation during your menstruation. Get massages. Take warm baths and embrace your body. Get moderate daily exercise. Buy clothes that fit. Accept compliments graciously, knowing that beauty on the outside reflects the beauty on the inside.

I like my body! And, it is 10-12 pounds heavier than I thought I could live with.

I do not see my body the way others do. The difference now is that I acknowledge my perceptions to be distorted by my low self-esteem, and let it sit at that. I recognize that I didn't "feel thin" at 85 pounds, so losing weight is not my answer anymore.

I am basically at peace with my weight. I do continue to weigh myself once daily, but when my weight fluctuates, I tell myself, it is okay and normal. I am healthy with this large body.

My physical body is a map, a reflection of the totality of every experience I have had since conception, and the genetic disposition of my family of origin!

My body image is based on my feelings about myself at that moment. How I see myself is based on my emotions. More and more now, I have times that I am at peace with my body image. I am glad I am healthy and not emaciated, as I used to be.

Most of my life I have used my body size to evaluate my self-worth. It wasn't until my mid-forties that I finally began to recognize that others valued me for who I was, not how I looked.

Practice Self-esteem!

When you try to improve yourself based on external standards, you will always question whether you are doing a good enough job. When you compare yourself with others, you are judging yourself relentlessly. When you are alienated from yourself because you want to please those around you, your life will feel empty inside. Bulimia is about this emptiness. It is a relentless symbolic quest to fill ourselves up, over and over again which, obviously, does not work.

The goal of recovery—and in fact the reward of recovery as well—is to know yourself well enough to "feel full" of yourself! You are an important, worthwhile human being, a source of compassion, creativity, love, wisdom, contentment, and happiness. For some reason, which you will surely discover in the process of recovery, you have become cut off from this knowledge, and don't even believe that it could be true! Without a foundation of self-awareness and self-love, however, nothing you do or buy or think will fill you up enough.

Therefore, the most important element to recovering from bulimia, or indeed any kind of personal "problem," is to raise your self-esteem. This means developing a relationship with your own inner self based on the conviction that you are a good person and deserve to have a happy life. In the past, you have thought poorly of yourself and what has it gotten you? An eating disorder! As one strong woman from our survey wrote, "I am a person, not a size!"

Self-esteem is not something that magically happens to you one day. It is something to practice, just like affirmations or writing. Get to know yourself. Take the time to listen to your inner voice. Be your own best friend. Think of the characteristics that are important in a best friend: respect, honesty, trust, compassion, thoughtfulness, humor, sensitivity, understanding, forgiveness, and unconditional love. If you practice approaching yourself with these qualities, they will become second nature.

My value as a human being is not about my size.

My bulimia was a symptom of very poor self-esteem, feelings of guilt, and helplessness. Through therapy, I learned how to treat myself with respect, that I control my own emotions, and to use frequent affirmations, which have turned my world around.

I have discovered at last how important I am as a person; a human that God created and loves. I realize that I am worthy of love and friendship; I deserve a good life, like everyone does.

As I became more comfortable with myself, I saw my life change in many ways. I found myself surrounded by friends who really liked me. And they were happy people, not miserable and depressed like my old friends. I have learned how to say "no" to people, and earned a lot of respect for doing so.

My self-concept has changed with recovery! I no longer have a secret life that I am utterly ashamed of! I no longer hate myself for continuing destructive behavior that does nothing but temporarily alleviate pain. I now love myself. I am a good person. Sometimes life is scary, but I can face it head-on now, instead of hiding in food.

I have found happiness. Once I stopped using food to cope with life, I started getting to know myself. To my delight, I like the person I discovered, and now I enjoy life.

I never dreamed I could like myself this much!

Intimacy

Secrecy and isolation are part of a bulimic's lifestyle. The primary relationship is with food, rather than the inner self or other people. Therefore, it should come as no surprise that recovery means breaking down the barriers to intimacy and learning how to develop healthy, caring relationships.

Once you become more comfortable with yourself, you will feel more comfortable with others, and vice versa. One enhances the other. For this reason, finding people to confide in can be crucial, especially for someone whose boundaries are unclear and who has been hurt in the past. Therapists are good choices, because they know how to guide, teach, challenge, and love when needed. A willing friend or relative can be a safe sounding board. Help can also be found in support groups with people who have faced or are facing similar problems. The important thing is to interact with others who will mirror your earnest effort to love and be loved.

Gradually and gently, allow more people to know who you really are. You might be amazed at how supportive some can be. As you gather the confidence to express your thoughts, feelings, and needs, you will be able to tackle relationships with some of the more difficult people in your life. Be aware of old, restrictive roles, and especially do not allow yourself to be abused. Separation and independence is a better choice than being misunderstood or mistreated.

Sometimes bulimia is used to avoid the intimacy of sexual relationships in response to sexual victimization, ranging from rape to the objectification of women in a male-dominated society. It is a way to have predictable physical pleasure alone. Gorging and purging is similar to the act and feelings of sexual intercourse—the slow build-up of intensity, the emotional craving for love, the stroking of the body, the explosion of physical pleasure/pain, and for some, a conditioned guilt. However, recovery creates the opportunity for having all kinds of love in your life. As you increase your self-esteem and your capacity for intimacy, you will be more ready and capable of having satisfying sexual relationships, as well.

Because most of us who have bulimia are ashamed of our behavior, we tend to hide, and keep our addiction a secret. We isolate from the ones who care and want to help us. There were many times I wanted to go to someone for help, but fear of rejection kept me isolated. I can't tell you what a relief it was when my secret was finally out in the open, and everyone who knows has been very supportive and understanding.

Being the child of an alcoholic father, and having been molested, I didn't feel that I had any control over my body until I discovered that I could control what and how much I ate. Basically, I think I wanted to be super thin in order to avoid getting close to guys.

Eating can be very sexual. I'm sure it's not coincidence, but I never had an orgasm until I stopped purging. Purging was almost a type of oral masturbation.

I found it a real challenge to let my friends know about my problem. Thinking of their reactions was scary, but, as long as I kept my secret, I couldn't get close to them. To most of them, I had everything—good grades, lots of dates. Little did they know that inside I was feeling inadequate, insecure and suffering from low self-esteem. I felt so stressed that I gradually began to pull myself back, leaving myself lonely, to binge and purge in peace. At first, I felt better. Later, I felt crazy. I started to socialize again, and this time, I chose a couple of friends who I thought I could trust with my secret. Their reactions were the very opposite of what I had feared—they were understanding and supportive, offering to help me in any way they could. I was so relieved. The acceptance gave me more confidence, and made it easier for me to tell other people. Not everyone had the same caring response, but I was able to accept that. I have no regrets about telling anyone. In fact, one of my closest, life-long friends shared that she was suffering from the same disease. We were able to be there for one another in a way we never had before.

Getting Past Food Fears

Every individual with bulimia has acquired myths and rules about eating and food, which manifest in symbolic eating patterns. Straying too far from these patterns is frightening because of the feelings they are hiding. We also label foods good or bad, usually based on their ability to add weight, and call ourselves good or bad when we eat them. Obviously, we will be afraid of those foods which make us feel bad or which have the power to spin us out of control.

In fact, there are no good and bad foods. Some foods are more nutritious than others, and it might be helpful for you to read up on basic nutrition. This will help you identify a variety of foods with which you might feel safe. Allowing yourself safe food will establish a "can-have," rather than a "can't-have" mentality. The negative associations that you attach to foods can be recognized and eliminated, especially if they are tackled head on in a systematic and determined manner. Do not belittle this challenge! For all the insight into the "whys" of your bulimia, the fact remains that you want to be able to eat without fear. Some situations will be harder to handle than others. You may even have setback binges. At those times, remember that you are going through a process. Take advantage of the situation to practice patience and determined self-inquiry. Food is *not* the enemy.

There are many things you can do to get past food fears. Replace the concept of dieting with eating for health. Experiment with (even a taste of) different foods and cuisines. A little risk-taking can result in feelings of competence and mastery. Try "gentle eating" and appreciating what you eat, instead of gobbling down your meals in a mindless trance. Affirm that you deserve to eat the best, and that there is plenty. Allow someone else to cook and serve a meal for you. Grocery shop with a friend and see what foods they like. Talk about your concerns. Try cooking with reverence or serving with style! Does this sound like an advertisement? I'm trying to sell you on eating and enjoying it!

I told myself that there will always be cheesecake or chocolate, bread, whatever! If I don't eat it now it won't be gone forever.

I allow myself anything I want, but in moderation. I have cake and ice cream, bread and butter, even cream in my coffee. The serving size is appropriate to my needs at the time. Being able to allow myself anything to eat has taken away the guilt, where before one bite of a "forbidden food" would lead to a binge. I eat it, enjoy it, and keep it down.

There are no forbidden foods for me. Certain foods don't have the power over me that I once gave them.

I try to eat several times a day in small portions. The foods that I eat now leave me feeling satisfied and I have no desire to binge.

Allowing myself all foods in small quantities has helped me, although I must remind myself I "deserve" cakes, cookies, etc. Cutting out all sugars set me up to binge, which reinforced that I was "bad" and couldn't control myself. I pretended not to eat sugar and carbohydrates, only to binge on them in private. I now eat sweets in small amounts in front of everyone, not trying to be "perfect" in my diet.

Health is my priority, not thinness.

CHAPTER 6

Things to Do Instead of Bingeing

An eating disorder takes up time, energy and money. These suggestions for things to do instead of bingeing have helped many people who answered the surveys. They can help you, too! The next time you are about to binge, or have already started bingeing, pick one idea from the "Immediate" list below, and do it! Use the "Short-term" list, following, for planning how not to binge in the future, and the "Long-term" list for gaining tools that will assist in your recovery process.

Immediate

• Call a safe friend and explain your problem. Cultivate more friends who are sensitive, compassionate, and capable of uplifting you. Sometimes it is good to talk to someone who has worked at overcoming an eating disorder.

• Postpone the binge for 15 minutes. Set your timer. Brush your teeth.

• Soak binge food in water.

• In panic situations, relax with deep breathing on the spot. Then, think it through: What am I feeling? Can I handle what's going on? Am I safe? Then do what you need to do.

• Get your mind on something else. Chew a piece of sugarless gum, turn on the radio, leave the environment that's tempting you to binge.

• Get some physical activity. Punch a boxing bag or scream into a pillow. Beat your bed with a tennis racket. If you've got a playmate, wrestle, do sports, play tag! Give that body some healthy expression! Crying can be a great release.

• Stop yourself and identify the real hunger. Write down your most spontaneous answers. These are your legitimate wants and needs.

• Write in your journal or tape record thoughts about your last night's dreams. Be intimate and honest. Look back at earlier entries to discover patterns and see progress. Address questions like, "What's the pay-off to this binge?"

• List the foods you are fantasizing about, seal the pieces in an envelope, and throw it away.

• Create and use panic cards with step-by-step instructions on what to do in difficult situations.

• If you can, stop yourself in the middle of a binge. This may seem impossible, but those who have done it say it is a very powerful accomplishment. Try to breathe peace into your very full body. I strongly suggest getting support with the different feelings that can arise with this exercise.

Short-term

• Make your own list of immediate things to do instead of bingeing.

• Pamper yourself with a facial, massage, new clothes, or hot bath. Take care of that body instead of abusing it.

• Relax with yoga, meditation, or other technique. Let your mind become still and your emotions calm.

• Give yourself permission to eat what you crave, but do it with a capable support person who understands your goal is to increase self-awareness, not to binge. Spend time talking about your feelings or writing them down.

• Write a letter to a family member about your bulimia. Write several letters over an extended period of time to the same person. You don't have to send any until you are ready.

• Talk to your mother and/or father about your childhood. Get up the courage to ask them about some of those moments of your past that have never been clear to you. Be prepared for a change in your relationship.

• Contact a childhood friend whom you have thought about but have not seen for some time. Catch up on each others' lives. They will not judge you for your bulimia; they have their own unique stories to tell.

• Eat what you consider "normal" for a day, then observe yourself and notice what you do and how it feels.

• Go to a cultural activity (concert, art show, museum, theater, etc.). Familiarize yourself with the subject before you go.

• Make lists about your life: things you like and dislike, your goals, needs, priorities, accomplishments or anything which helps you get to know yourself and feel better about your life.

• Practice saying no—it is your fundamental human right. It also gets easier after the first few times! You are the one who knows your limits and boundaries. Be assertive and express your needs, small or large. It may feel risky, but try it anyway!

• Get busy with some project immediately after eating a normal meal.

• Take a vacation. Get away from your usual routine, and decide not to binge and purge while away.

• Try visual imagery. It is very effective to see yourself doing something before you do it. Picture yourself mentally going into your kitchen and eating a healthy meal, cleaning up, and walking out of the kitchen.

• Mark your calendar with a big star every day you do not binge or purge.

Long-term

• Try not to be so perfect. Bulimics are often tidy about every aspect of their lives except their own inner peace. The verge of a binge feels very imperfect. Don't worry about housework or studying for a while. Don't wear make-up and see how it feels.

• Get involved in volunteer work for a worthwhile cause. See your own goodness radiated back to you.

• Learn something new: a foreign language, CPR, a musical instrument, an art medium, some kind of mechanics or electronics, computers, or how to ride a motorcycle! Try out some classes which emphasize self-reliance, assertiveness, or improved body image.

• Think about a new way to make money instead of obsessing about food, and then follow through on your scheme. This can be a hobby or a new job!

• Use positive language. Try saying out loud that you are a nice person and deserve to live happily. Talk into a tape recorder. Repeat affirmations.

• Read! Go to the library or local bookstore. Always have a book to read for pleasure (novel, biography, history, etc.).

• Buy a pet! It's a great way to practice love! A humble, little dog will provide unconditional acceptance, companionship, something to love and care for, and a reason to take walks, which provide relaxation, exercise, and an opportunity to get out of the house without having to feel alone.

CHAPTER 7

Advice for Loved Ones

A few words from Leigh:

Lindsey and I fell in love at first sight. Shortly after we acknowledged that love, she told me she had a "horrible" secret. I was a bit relieved that the big problem was *only an eating disorder.* When she fully described the scope of her bulimia, however, I realized that I had underestimated its seriousness. I responded to her disclosure with love and compassion, vowing to help her in recovery.

I quickly discovered that there was no instantaneous cure for Lindsey's bulimia, and we both feared that unless she gave it up, our love was jeopardized. It monopolized her time and attention, and prevented her from appreciating the love and beauty within herself that I recognized so immediately. I became willing to do anything to help her, and she allowed me to be supportive.

Lindsey's battle with bulimia was our primary focus for many months as she worked to put it behind her. During that time, I continually reminded myself that freeing herself of the food problems was completely up to her. I could make suggestions, be a sounding board, or even take punches with the boxing gloves, but I was not the one who had to do the work. Of course, I was not merely a unaffected bystander—our union was predicated on her recovery. Also, her struggles forced me to examine my own values on such subjects as family relationships, weightism, stereotypes in the media, feminism, and healthy eating. Still, I never lost sight of the fact that she was the one in crisis. Happily, it has now been well over a decade since Lindsey recovered from bulimia, and love has filled our lives.

Over the years, we have worked to help others overcome their eating disorders. Parents and loved ones often ask me what they can do, and I usually make these recommendations:

• Remember that she (or he) has the food problem, and it is up to them to do the work.

• Make a pact of complete honesty.

• Be patient, sympathetic, non-judgemental, and a good listener.

• Allow her to establish reasonable rules and goals about food and eating, but assert your own rights as well.

• Make clear that she is responsible for the consequences of bulimic behavior. For example: If she eats all the food in the house, she should replace it using her own money.

• If she binges, she should face it afterwards by talking about why it happened, writing in a journal, or exploring options for how to avoid bingeing the next time she is in a similar situation.

• Recognize that she has the right to make her own decisions, and that she uses bulimia as a substitute for confronting painful feelings or experiences.

• Do not allow meals to be a battleground. For most bulimics, food is not the main issue, and sometimes looking past the immediate situation can illuminate deeper issues.

• Let her be responsible for her recovery, and do not constantly check up on her unless she asks that of you.

• Be open to the possibility that you are contributing in some way to her problem, and that you might need to change some of your behaviors and beliefs.

• Be compassionate. Recovering bulimics are facing a lot of painful feelings. They may even be getting in touch with previously repressed memories of past traumas. They need your love and support at these times more than ever.

• Learn about eating disorders and related issues such as: social pressures on women, the exploitation of thinness, family dynamics, and self-esteem.

• Work with a professional therapist, and be available for joint-counseling sessions.

On our survey we asked, "What can family and friends do to help?" The responses provide excellent guidelines:

The best way for loved ones to help me is just love me, and be there when I need them.

Be honest and supportive of the person finding a cure, though not supporting the behavior.

Look at how you feel about food, or if you contribute to your friend's or loved-one's bulimia.

I'm firmly convinced that loved ones first need to admit that this is a serious problem, and that it takes a great deal of sometimes unpleasant work for the bulimic to get better.

Communication is very important! The person who is bulimic needs to be able to freely discuss any feelings and concerns that she might have, without feeling threatened.

Loved ones can encourage, love, support, and actively listen. I found that some people listen for about sixty seconds, and then interject their opinions and prejudices instead of openly listening and really hearing what is said.

They can de-emphasize food, and support the concept that a woman is beautiful even if she weighs more than a model. Models are not the standard of beauty.

Be there for me! Isolation and loneliness just worsen the problem. Help me to build self-esteem and self-worth. Notice the good things and comment on them instead of harping on the bad.

Loved ones need to help bulimics assert themselves. I needed reassurance that it was okay to say "no" to people.

Recognize that the bulimic's perfectionism and conscientiousness hides a deep sense of inferiority and self-doubt. Draw her out of her "authoritarian cocoon." Speak your mind!

Try to learn about the disorder, especially the underlying issues and causes.

Encourage the bulimic to go into therapy.

Be patient and do not expect "instant" results.

Offer to pay for therapy!

My loved ones can best help me by showing their love for me both in words and actions. I especially need to know they love me in spite of my bingeing and purging. Please don't lecture me or tell me

I'm sick. I know loving me isn't easy, but please try! I need your love! I need to be accepted and smiled at.

Never make a big deal about food. Food is not the main issue, and the sooner the family realizes this, the sooner they can help a bulimic realize it as truth.

CHAPTER 8

A Two-Week Program to Stop Bingeing

The purpose of this section is to give bulimics specific goals and tasks to help them stop abusing food. By following this program, you will get the experience of wellness. It is not an instant cure, but is rather like an instant support group! It can also provide insights into the recovery process for those readers who are interested.

Read through the entire agenda to get an idea of what the assignments will be. Even if you are not ready to start the course, you can benefit from trying some of the techniques without following the daily routine. We recommend the same things that we talk about in this book; journal writing, relaxation, moderate exercise, professional therapy, talking to people, etc. Once you've read the program through, you'll have lots of thoughts and inspiration to stop bingeing.

The course requires spending time and effort. You will practice having fun, being loving, thinking happy thoughts, and getting to know yourself. These can be a habit, too! If you use this plan faithfully, you may not binge for two weeks, and you will have more skills and confidence to help you stop your bulimia for good. If you do binge, you have not failed. You are given criteria to understand what has happened, and guidelines to prevent the next binge. We are providing a framework for your recovery. We'll hold your hand by supporting you with our suggestions and our "presence," but you must do the work.

Let us remind you again that your bulimia has served you in many ways, most notably to protect you from painful feelings. Experiencing past hurts, present shame, or any other unfamiliar, unexpressed feelings can be frightening and overwhelming. Moreover, if you are not used to having feelings or even differentiating one from another, you may be tempted to turn to your familiar friend, bulimia, for safety. Can you understand how natural this is? Can you have compassion for yourself given the task ahead of you?

Our advice is to be aware and be prepared. If you are not yet in therapy, have someone or something to support you—a friend, relative, hotline, cassette tapes of your own soothing voice, special music, books on feelings, or a notebook.

DAY 1
My life is better without bulimia!

Hooray! You are making a commitment to end your bulimia, and you'll be happy that you did! Since this is your first day, we will have orientation. In the future, the instructions will not include as many details. If Day 1 begins in the afternoon, do everything anyway. But tomorrow, you will need to start at the beginning of the day. Be prepared to spend some money for materials and field trips. These costs are generally low, and by the end of the course you will have saved money that you probably would have spent on food.

Today, buy a three-ring notebook, five dividers, and paper specifically for this course. Keep it and this book next to your bed, and as soon as you get up in the morning, turn to the appropriate page and get started.

First Things First: Every day, as soon as you can, but definitely before eating, you have a few things to do (in order): Read the Thought for the Day, do the Morning Warmup, read the entire day's plan in this book, and work in your notebook.

IMPORTANT NOTE: This program offers you the experience of freedom from bulimia. This is *not* a test. There is no right or wrong way to do it. Stick to it faithfully or choose activities and give them a try.

Thought for the Day: My life is better without bulimia!
Keep repeating this thought over and over all day. Say it to yourself when you sit down and when you stand up, when you open doors, while driving, while washing your hands, twice when you eat, etc. Every day you will be given another thought. Say it with conviction and belief, and most of all, repeat it!

The Morning Warmup: If you have to go to the bathroom, you may. If you have roommates, husbands, kids, or others that require your attention, make them wait, participate, or support you in any way necessary to afford you this short bit of time.
Today, let's start with a good stretch. It will take about ten minutes. Put on some music, if you wish. Here are some hints for getting the most from stretching:
1. Instead of copying someone else's routine, make up your own as you go along. Unlearn rules about keeping joints straight or repetitions.
2. Don't bounce or try to be flexible. Relax and enjoy feeling your muscles. Touch them with your fingers.
3. Groan, sigh, laugh, and breathe noisily—it's fun and releases tension.
4. Slowly, stretch your whole body.

5. If you feel tension in your face, there is tension in your body—relax your face!

6. Don't overstretch. If it starts to hurt, relax, breathe, and don't push yourself to go further than you can. Stretching should feel good!

7. Give yourself about ten minutes. Include your eyes, neck, back, shoulders, chest, arms, fingers, thighs, calves, and feet. Alternate bending and arching your back, twisting one direction and then the other, etc. Also, remember to keep repeating the Thought for the Day.

Your Notebook

Every day there will be assignments of things to write about, places to go, or exercises to do. Do them any time, before or after meals, instead of bingeing, whenever you can. We strongly suggest that you do all of the assignments, but there may be times when you cannot. Do each day's work that day, and if necessary, catch up afterwards.

Arrange your notebook with five dividers labeled: Journal, Options, Binge, Written Homework, and Other. Today, we will explain about each section:

Journal: Sometimes you will be given journal writing assignments, but you should also use this space whenever you have something to say. Always copy the Thought for the Day into your journal.

Today's Options: Every day we will provide a few suggestions for things you can do instead of bingeing. You should also write some of your own ideas. Emphasize techniques that work. One requirement of this course is that you consult this list if you are on the verge of a binge.

Binge: Reward yourself with a sheet in this section when you resist the temptation to binge. You might describe how you felt not bingeing, what options worked for you, or glue in a photo that expresses your feelings, or words of wisdom that may have inspired or entertained you that day.

What if you do binge? Don't give up! Would you quit school if you received a poor grade on one assignment? No, you would realize that more study is necessary. HERE IS YOUR EXTRA HOMEWORK IF YOU HAVE BINGED:

1. Write about the binge. You may include answers to some of these questions: What led you to do the binge? What were your thoughts before and during? What did you eat? Did you purge? How? What were you feeling? Did you try to do something instead of bingeing? Why didn't that work? What else could you have done? What will you try to do instead of bingeing next time the cravings are so strong?

2. Glue in a photo that reminds you of the binge. Some ideas: cut out a magazine advertisement for junk food and put a big black X over it, write over a diet advertisement with the words "Weight is not important to me, loving myself is!" or a news clipping that reminds you that you are still better off than some unfortunate people.

3. Spend ten minutes relaxing. See Today's Option #2.

Written Homework: This notebook section will be for keeping your written assignments.

Other: This section is for any additional writing, clippings, souvenirs, etc. Be sure to stock your notebook with plenty of paper and attach a couple of extra pens or pencils to the inside cover so they will always be handy. It's a good idea to carry a notepad wherever you go, just in case you have an inspiring idea to record.

Today's Options:

1. Punch, kick, yell, and go wild! Use an appropriate object, such as beds and pillows, boxing bags, or willing friends. Vent your frustrations and tensions, and loudly express those feelings which you've been swallowing. Look at a clock and go three rounds of two minutes each. Make that pillow feel your anger, beat the #$&!! out of it!

2. Get away, quick! Go to a quiet restful place where food is not easily available, such as a park, beach, museum, church, or library. Bring your notebook and write in your journal. Use the relaxation or meditation techniques described in the "Relax, Relax, Relax" section of Chapter 5 in this book.

3. Work on today's homework.

4. Exercise! Be sure to stretch first, and pace yourself—don't over-exert. If you have a favorite way of exercising, do that. Otherwise, lightly jog and walk for an hour, or take a long bicycle ride. Isn't that about how long you might spend on a binge?

5. Make a list of three options of your own, and do one of those.

Homework: Day 1

1. Write about your bingeing habits of the last week, month, and years. Include frequency of binges and purges, and describe in detail your last binge. You will refer to this assignment later during the course, so be sure to leave it in the "Written Homework" section.

2. Write a final journal entry before going to sleep tonight. Include what you did today, how you felt, and some reflections on this course. Be sure to write, "My life is better without bulimia!" Life really is better without it.

Good Night: If today was hard for you, stick to it, because as the days progress, the program will help you stop bingeing. Even if we haven't met personally, we want you to know that we love you and completely support your efforts. We encourage you to write us about your experiences, and we will write back! Remember to read Day 2 as soon as you wake up, but rest with the knowledge that you are worthwhile, strong, and you're going to make it! Sleep well.

DAY 2
Look for solutions, not problems

Good morning! We hope you slept well. If you are excited about this course to end your bulimia, great! Let's get started.

First Things First: Read the Thought for the Day, do the Morning Warmup, read the entire day's plan, and then write a short journal entry (see below).

Thought for the Day: Look for solutions, not problems.

It's your mind that creates problems. It can create anything, abundance or scarcity, happiness or worry. Notice your belittling thoughts and get rid of them. You are not unworthy, you just think that you are. Today, look on the bright side; in other words, look for solutions, not problems!

The Morning Warmup: Take a long, hot shower or bath. By all means, sing at least one song out loud. Gently stretch and massage yourself as you bathe. Think about what we've planned for you to do today, what you will write about in your journal, and what will be acceptable for you to eat for breakfast.

Short Journal Entry: Describe one of the happiest moments of your life. Try to remember why you felt so good about yourself then. We want you to remember that good feeling throughout the day.

Today's Options:

1. Gather your binge food and soak it with water in the sink. Don't concern yourself with the waste, you would have wasted it by purging.

2. Take another shower or bath, repeating everything that you did in the Morning Warmup.

3. Drink water or eat a carrot.

4. Tell yourself to slow down. Spend fifteen to thirty minutes in deep relaxation or meditation.

5. Review yesterday's options and your own list. Choose something that will work!

6. Work on Today's Assignments.

Homework: Day 2

1. Write answers to these questions: What are your bulimia goals for these two weeks? For after the course? What are your goals for today? What kind of meals do you want to eat? How much food would make you feel good about yourself? What do you want to do immediately after breakfast?

2. Begin compiling your SUPPORT LIST. Make one list of all the people who already know about your bulimia. Make another list of everyone you will tell. This list should include practically everyone who is close to you. You will not be contacting these people yet, so there will be some time to get used to this idea.

Now, make a loose order of those you will contact first, second, etc. Include the people who already know. Next to their names, indicate the probable method of contact that you will use, such as: phone calls, letters, in-person, etc. Getting support is one way of looking for solutions.

3.   Today, begin thinking about something new you want to learn. This learning will not have to end at the completion of these two weeks. Some ideas: yoga, a musical instrument, a foreign language, figure drawing, CPR, skydiving, etc. You will be required to spend some time on this, so it should be a fun activity for you.

4.   Go for a one hour walk in your neighborhood. Weather is no obstacle, a brisk walk in the rain or snow can be invigorating. Bring your notepad to record any ideas that you have during the walk. Stop to smell the roses! Smile and talk to people you see, look them in the eye. Observe everything, even the sky. Do not eat or go into any stores during this walk.

IMPORTANT NOTE: We often recommend that you get away, but when you return it is equally important to maintain the feelings that kept you from bingeing. As soon as you return home, sit quietly for five minutes and relax. After that, write in your journal. Other options are to call someone, drink a cup of hot tea, take a shower or bath, or do whatever else works for you. As helpful as it is to get away, it is crucial to maintain your positive feelings and actions upon return.

Good night: You may be experiencing some joy and sense of accomplishment. You may be frustrated and anxious. Regardless of how it went, another day has passed. Reaffirm that you will continue this course of recovery. You can do it! You are doing it! As you drift off to sleep tonight, remember that moment of happiness we asked you to write about earlier. Put yourself in that situation, feel the warmth and love. Somewhere nearby, we are there, too, thinking of you as a wonderful, loving person. Sweet dreams!

DAY 3
Lighten up!

Today is going to be a fun day. Everyone has a sense of humor, but sometimes life's pressures prevent us from having a good laugh. Today, laugh! It feels great! Rearrange your schedule if necessary to get the most enjoyment out of today's assignments.

First Things First: Read the Thought for the Day, do the Morning Warmup, read the entire day's plan in this book, and review the options in your notebook.

Thought for the Day: Lighten up! (This has nothing to do with your weight!)

The Morning Warmup: Bring a watch or clock into the bathroom with you and lock the door. Spend no less than five minutes looking at your face in the mirror. The longer, the better. Try not to look away. Make extended eye contact with yourself. Who is that? When is the last time you really looked at your face? Look at all of the colors in your eyes, did you ever notice that before? When you look at someone else, on what do you base your judgments? What kinds of judgments do you make about yourself? How about making some positive affirmations about yourself instead?

Make dopey faces in the mirror. Stretch your face, wiggle your lips, squish your nose, pull on your ears, etc. Grunt, squeak, say "Ho ho ho," "ha ha ha," and "he he he." Laugh out loud, even if it's a phony laugh. Come on, lighten up, really get silly!

While you're in the bathroom, talk out loud to your scale. (See Today's Homework #5.) Tell it that you resent its influence over you. Have a good heart-to-heart with it!

Today's Options:

1. Write affirmations in your journal 50 times, such as: "I trust myself," "I won't binge today," or "Every day in every way I'm getting better and better." As long as you are still tempted to binge, keep writing!

2. Go for a walk.

3. Do one of today's assignments. There's a lot to do today.

4. Review what has worked and been suggested before.

Homework: Day 3

1. Go to a bookstore today to do these first two homework assignments. Look for books that will help you start your new learning project, which was mentioned in yesterday's homework. Buy one if you're ready.

2. At the bookstore, read through joke books. Laugh out loud right there in the bookstore. Spend no time in the "diet" or "cooking" sections unless they are part of your study project. If you're really ambitious, also go to a record or video store and buy or rent a comedy recording.

3. Contact someone from your support list to tell some of the new jokes that you read today. This conversation isn't necessarily the time to talk about your bulimia, but that would be okay, too.

4. Write a letter to the first "letter" person on your support list. You do not have to send it.

5. Stop weighing yourself so often. If you can, destroy your home scale! A hammer will work just fine, though running over it with a car may be equally satisfying. Don't just throw it away. Destroy it and laugh.

Good night: We hope that this day has been as enjoyable for you as it has been for us. We got a couple of good giggles from the plan. Did you?

DAY 4
I can eat without fear!

You may have noticed that we haven't said much about food or eating yet. Today, we will! Whatever the cause of your bulimia—whether it be family, society, chemical imbalance, karma, a desire to be thin, or anything else—you will need to eat. Don't wait to understand all your "whys" because that in itself will not stop you from bingeing. Appreciate food for its taste and nourishment, and let go of your negative, obsessive thoughts.

First Things First: Read the Thought for the Day, do the Morning Warmup, read the entire day's plan in this book, and do the short journal entry which is assigned.

Thought for the Day: I can eat without fear.

The Morning Warmup: Do a short, five minute stretch. If you need to refresh your memory about stretching, re-read the guidelines from Day 1.

Morning Journal Entry: Plan today's menu. Include breakfast, lunch, dinner, snacks, and a small, acceptable dessert. Be specific, you will go shopping for groceries later. Your meals today should be balanced, tasty, and non-threatening. Stick to this menu faithfully.

Today's Options:
1.   Buy a plant or new pet, such as a goldfish or turtle.
2.   Call someone from your support list.
3.   Work on your new study project or today's assignments.
4.   Ask yourself: What's the payoff to bingeing? How does that compare with the satisfaction of not bingeing? Then, just don't do it!
5.   As always, review the other days' options.

Homework: Day 4
1.   Take the first few names from the support list you compiled on Day 2. If you plan on talking to them, draft some of the sentences first. Include questions that you want to ask, and specific things that you want them to do for you. It is important to have a support person to call when you are craving a binge.
2.   You need to go grocery shopping. Make a detailed list and buy only the food you need for the menu that you have prepared. Do not buy anything that is not on your list. Stick to your menu. You can do it!
3.   Bring your notepad to the grocery. In it, write down the name and price of every item of food that you would eat on a binge. Then take the list and either burn it, tear it up, or eat it!
4.   Have a special meal today. Eat by candlelight, with soft music, or with good china. Practice gentle eating. Put your utensil down between bites, taste your food, savor each bite.

Good night: Many people say that food is not the issue for bulimics. But while we agree with this in principal, we still emphasize that reformed eating habits are crucial for recovery. The binge-purge behavior was learned, now it must be unlearned. Let your friends help you, and believe in yourself. Stick to this program! Even if we've never met you, we care about you, we really do.

DAY 5
Think lovely thoughts!

The suggestions that we make day-to-day require you to work all day, not just for a few moments while you read the page or do an assignment. The actual assignments are secondary to the effort that you put into them. You are setting the goals and following through. Think about them as you eat, rest, bathe, walk, talk, etc. When faced with pressure and temptation, be strong and fight. Beat the feathers out of that pillow, soak the binge food, get away, seek help from those who truly love you. You are worthwhile and would help them if they needed it. Now you need help. Ask for and accept it.

First Things First: Read the Thought for the Day, do the Morning Warmup, read the entire day's plan in this book, and write in your journal.

Thought for the Day: Think lovely thoughts.

See the positive, in everyone and everything. If you begin to have a negative thought, stop and replace it with a positive one. Consciously and actively practice feelings of love, approval, and confidence.

The Morning Warmup: See yourself a little differently. Spend about twenty minutes doing this relaxation exercise: In a quiet place, lie flat on your back, eyes closed. You will tense and then relax every part of your body. Start with your toes and feet, flexing them, holding the tension, and then releasing, allowing that area to gently relax. Follow this procedure up your calves, knees, thighs, buttocks, genitals, waist, chest, back, shoulders, arms, etc. By the time you have rested your entire body, spend a few minutes imagining yourself without judgment as: tremendously fat, skinny, tall, a midget, different races, the opposite sex, and pure light without form.

Morning Journal Entry: Write one sentence each about five to ten good things in your life.

Today's Options:

1. Count how much money you saved yesterday by not buying binge food. Think of an enjoyable way to use that amount of money, then go ahead and spend it!

2. Work with diligence on your study project.

3. Review past options.

Homework: Day 5

1. Write a physical description of yourself. Include what you saw in the mirror yesterday when you studied your face, your hands, skin complexion and texture, hair, legs, etc. Who do you look like? What are some judgments you've made about your body? Do you wish that there were differences? What are they? Are they reasonable or even possible?

2. Buy a women's mass market magazine. When you get home, go through the ads, articles, and photos. Tear out everything that appeals to or depicts thin women, food, diets, or beautifying products, such as cosmetics. How much of the magazine is left? Why is the torn out pile so large? Reflect on the economics and message of the medium in your journal. Tear the junk pile to shreds, while you repeat today's Thought for the Day.

3. Whenever you have a negative thought today, write it down, then tear up the paper. Replace the thought with a positive one!

4.   IMPORTANT: Review the plan for Day 9. You will be going on an all-day excursion. You may have to do some rearranging of your schedule and planning ahead, so start today. You might want to contact a friend to accompany you.

5.   Allow yourself a small dessert tonight. Do not obsess about it, merely select and eat your sweet as a reward for your efforts to end your bulimia. Do not count calories. If you begin to even think negative thoughts after eating your dessert, immediately stop what you are doing and write your thoughts in your journal. Then spend ten or fifteen minutes stretching or going for a walk.

Good night: Words, whether spoken or thought, have tremendous power. The way that we verbalize something is how we perceive it. If negative words are used, negative feelings surface. Any event can be thought of in many different ways. Rarely will two people have an identical impression of the same event. You may have gotten used to thinking of yourself as bulimic, worthless, unlovable, or unattractive. You must change those thoughts. Think of yourself as deserving of love and beautiful on the inside.

DAY 6
I can accept support from others

We hope you had sweet dreams from your lovely thoughts of yesterday. Keep practicing and looking on the bright side.

First Things First: Read the Thought for the Day, do the Morning Warmup, read the entire day's plan in this book, and work in your notebook.

Thought for the Day: I can accept support from others.

Getting support does not mean only having horribly serious talks. A support relationship can be fun for both people. By asking someone to help you stop bingeing and purging, you are being honest, respecting that person's point-of-view, and deepening the bonds of friendship. What could be better than that? You have many new experiences from this program alone. Share them!

The Morning Warmup: Loosen up with a quick, five minute stretch, followed by a long, hot shower. If you have any body oil, splash it on!

Today's Options:

1. Talk to a neighbor. Even casual conversation can distract you from bingeing.

2. Pamper your pets or plants.

3. Consult your own list and pick one of the first three ideas.

Homework: Day 6

1. Review your support list and pick one local person. Tell them that you have something important to talk about tonight, and also ask them to go with you to a movie. Television is okay as a second choice. Meet at least an hour or two before the show starts to have enough time to talk about your bulimia. Follow that with some good clean fun! If you have a previous commitment that cannot be broken, schedule this for the first available night. Make plans now!

2. Begin to arrange for at least one session of professional therapy. Re-read the answers to "How should I choose a therapist?" in Chapter 1. At the very least, make a list of therapists.

3.   Confront your feelings about family members. Choose one member of your family, and then write about how they have affected you in the following ways (we'll use Mom as an example. You may pick anyone): During your lifetime, what negative thing has Mom said or done that you remember? How did you feel? How did you react? Why has this event stuck with you? What do you wish you had said or done at the time? What could she have said or done to convey her message in a more positive manner? Could the two of you have talked? Is it worth talking about now?

4.   Continue writing about your family and how they can support you. Answer these questions: How do they support you now? Are they doing their best? What can you do to improve your relationship with your family?

5.   Talk to a family member about your bulimia recovery.

Good night: Was the movie good? Was it as entertaining as your conversation with your support person? We bet that you are a pretty likable person after all! Of the hundreds of people who have confessed their bulimia to us—we are sometimes the first ones told—each one has been sensitive, sincere, pleasant, and usually able to joke. Great qualities!

DAY 7
Peace of Mind

Today you will be half-way through this program to stop bingeing. Think about it for a moment. Have your binges decreased this week? Most of the course emphasis so far has been on getting to know yourself better. Next week, we will encourage you to interact more. Today, you deserve to take it a little easier, but that does not mean to slack off on your commitment to doing the homework and not bingeing.

First Things First: Read the Thought for the Day, do the Morning Warmup, read the entire day's plan in this book, and work in your notebook.

Thought for the Day: I deserve rest and relaxation.

Many bulimics are high-achievers and feel guilty if they are not being productive. Life is not a race or contest, and everyone needs to kick back at times. If bingeing has been a way for you to unwind or be entertained, you need new outlets.

The Morning Warmup: Use the progressive relaxation technique from Day 5. Today, when you are in that state of deep physical relaxation, visualize a special place. This can be somewhere that you know well, or it can be imagined. Put yourself there by seeing everything, hearing the sounds of that place, smelling the air, and feeling your entire being in that restful scene.

Today's Options:

1. Chew gum, a carrot, or a celery stick.
2. Flush what might have been your binge food down the toilet.
3. Repeat this morning's relaxation and return to your special place.
4. Review options that have worked before.

Homework: Day 7

1. Write or call someone you love. We recommend seeking out a person whom you have not seen for a long time, but care for, such as a childhood friend or lost relative.
2. Read the plan for Day 9, and make any necessary preparations.

3. Rest your mind by watching at least one hour of television, which can have a tranquilizing effect.

4. Work on your study project.

5. Today, avoid speaking whenever possible. Try to reflect more on your inner thoughts. Silence is wonderful!

Good night: We suggest that you get to bed early tonight, and enjoy a long sleep. Congratulations on sticking to the program for a week. It's all downhill from here!

DAY 8
Love Day!

Today is "Love Day" and you're going to love it! Last week we concentrated on inner growth. This week we will expand our horizons to include people, places, and outside experiences.

First Things First: Read the Thought for the Day, do the Morning Warmup, read the entire day's plan in this book, and write in your journal.

Thought for the Day: I love me.

If you think no one loves you, that your parents didn't, your friends don't, and you're sure that the "right" guy or gal won't, how can you love yourself? You must realize that you are the source of love. Love doesn't come from "out there."

The Morning Warmup: Take a sensual shower or hot bath. Don't just soak or wash, but massage your muscles. Appreciate the sensuality of your skin. Touch yourself with a lover's embrace. If your situation permits, share this experience.

Short Journal Entry: What is your definition of "love"?

Today's Options:

1. Let's review a few from last week: exercise, soak food, beat up a pillow, get away, drink water, read your joke book. Have you tried these yet?

2. Take a round-trip bus ride anywhere. Observe the people on the bus, practice seeing each of them through loving eyes. Do not eat on this trip!

3. Try prayer.

4. Go to a spot you love away from home, like a park, the beach, under a particular tree or overlooking a beautiful scene. Close your eyes, count your breaths, and relax.

Homework: Day 8

1. Do a good deed. Some possibilities: visit a nursing home and spend a little time talking to an elderly person, babysit for a friend with small children, visit someone and help them clean or cook, offer your services to a non-profit organization, etc. Don't just call or think about it. This is the main assignment today, go somewhere and do it!

2. Tell someone you love them.

3. Continue to work on these earlier assignments: arranging for professional therapy, and contacting people from your support list.

4. Have you lined up someone to join you on Day 9?

5. Throughout the day, look at your reflection in different mirrors and windows. Think about it. Does your mood depend on what you see?

6. To elicit feelings of love, listen to a favorite old song or piece of music, look through a scrapbook or photo album, write or call a friend you haven't seen in years.

Good night: Everyday can be a "Love Day" if you practice. Love is not something that comes from outside of yourself. As we wrote this book, feelings of love generated the words. Doing good deeds, helping others, feeling good about ourselves, these give us a purpose for living.

DAY 9
It's all right to be different

Invite someone to join you in today's activities. Role playing can be fun as well as revealing. We get too caught up in our identities and our own particular roles. We act in ways to please our parents, bosses, teachers, and friends. What about you? Do you live for others with little regard for your own feelings? Do you want to be thin to please a lover, parent, or society? Who makes judgments about you? Is it okay to be different from the norm? Don't be afraid of what people think, be fearless!

First Things First: Today, read the entire day's plan first. Then, read the Thought for the Day, do the Morning Warmup, and write in your journal.

Thought for the Day: It's all right to be different.

Today, you will be! Create a new identity for yourself and act it out! Of course, you must choose not to be bulimic. It doesn't have to be someone exotic, it might be what you consider to be a "normal" person.

The Morning Warmup: As you know by reading today's plan, you are going to pretend to be someone else today. Wash your hair and fix it a way that this other person would wear it, maybe with scarf, curls, parted in the middle, etc. Get dressed as this person would dress. If you usually wear pants, maybe you'll wear a skirt, and high heels. If you usually wear makeup, maybe this person won't. As you "put on your costume" begin to assume the new identity.

Morning Journal Entry: Write about the person you are pretending to be today. What's your name? What are your likes and dislikes? What's your background? What special talents do you have? What do you like to eat? Make your description interesting, and complete. Then become that person for the day.

Today's Options:

1.   The person you're pretending to be doesn't binge!
2.   Use your support person.
3.   Go to a busy intersection and people-watch. Notice how different everyone is.
4.   Buy a national newspaper or magazine. How many thin people are shown in pictures or ads? How many weight loss methods can you count? Rip it to shreds!

Homework: Day 9

1.   Today you will be going on an all-day excursion. If it is absolutely impossible for you to take the day off, then substitute this day for the earliest one possible.
2.   You've been instructed to read today's lesson and to invite a friend to join you. If you are doing it with a friend, warn them in advance that you are going to be "in character" and he or she could be, too. It may sound crazy and you might be slightly embarrassed to suggest it, but it will be fun for both of you.

Obviously, it will be difficult to continue this masquerade all day. Don't worry about it. Be that person as much as possible, and use this "distance" to get to know yourself better.

3. Leave your usual surroundings. Bring anything that the "pretend you" would bring. Even introduce yourself to people along the way as this other person. Have fun, go with it!

4. When you return home, sit quietly for five minutes and relax. After that, write in your journal. As helpful as it is to get away, it is crucial to maintain your positive feelings and actions upon return.

5. Write a journal entry: What aspects of your "make-believe" character do you want to keep for your own? Which aspects of "the real you" never changed?

Good night: Wherever you go, you can carry your old garbage with you or leave it behind—your choice!

DAY 10
Assert yourself!

Yesterday, we asked you to try being someone else. Now it's time to enjoy being who you are.

First Things First: Read the Thought for the Day, do the Morning Warmup, read the entire day's plan in this book, and work in your notebook.

Thought for the Day: I can assert myself!

Expose your feelings, opinions, and real self. It's okay if people don't always agree with you. It's okay if you don't always agree with them. You must learn to say "no" sometimes and set your own boundaries. This may mean choosing different friends or living situations. Be yourself!

The Morning Warmup: Have a good, long (15-30 minutes) stretch and/or exercise workout.

Today's Options:

1. Express a strong opinion. (For example, write a television network to complain about offensive programming.)

2. Say "NO!" out loud to bulimia.

3. Aggressively hammer nails, chop wood, or beat up a pillow.

4. Call a friend and share with each other your hopes and dreams for the future.

5. Donate canned food to a homeless shelter. Take cans from your pantry and do it.

Homework: Day 10

1. List 10-15 character traits you like about yourself.

2. Draw a self-portrait. (We'd like to see a copy!)

3. Talk to a family member about your recovery from bulimia.

4. Work on your study project. This has been something we have not said much about, other than to do it. If you have gotten into this project, it is already giving you great rewards.

Good night: Ten days is a long time to follow a regime such as ours. Congratulate yourself on getting this far, regardless of whether or not you've binged. As you lie in bed, feel the tension drift out of your body. The more time you spend away from bulimia, the better you will feel.

DAY 11
I can get what I want!

By recovering from bulimia, you are not changing into someone else. You are recognizing that you are good, after all. It's a subtle shift in perspective.

First Things First: Read the Thought for the Day, do the Morning Warmup, read the entire day's plan in this book, and write in your journal.

Thought for the Day: I can get what I want.

We already know that you do not want to be bulimic anymore; but what do you want? There are "wants" of a physical nature: I want a new car, I want to go on vacation, or I want to look attractive. There are also "wants" of an inner nature: I want to be happy, I want to love myself, or I want to feel attractive. Think about your wants.

The Morning Warmup: Go for a gentle jog of about 15 minutes. Be sure to stretch first. Do not run a race!

Today's Options:

1. Have a meal with a support person. Choose foods that you would really enjoy eating. Leave some on your plate and express thanks for the meal.

2. Go somewhere you've been wanting to go. Buy a souvenir.

3. Instead of bingeing, give yourself a treat. Do #2 of today's homework.

4. Write these words fifty times in your notebook, "I want to quit bulimia!"

Homework: Day 11

1. List fifty "I Wants!" including things you want to own, do, and feel. Pick five and make plans to achieve them.

2. Treat yourself to one candy bar or favorite "forbidden" food, and eat it in a special place. Any food is okay in

moderation. You have to practice permitting yourself to eat without overdoing it.

3. Buy yourself something with money you would have spent on food.

4. Make an appointment with a therapist, if you have not already done so.

5. Work a half an hour on your study project.

Good night: You've started to focus on some of your "wants." These are much healthier thoughts than obsessing about bingeing. Believe in yourself. Remember that you can get what you want, and add this one: "I am overcoming bulimia!"

DAY 12
Examining Values

Who you are is more important than how you look. Do you make judgments based on appearance alone? Should you? Today, let's find out!

First Things First: Read the Thought for the Day, read the entire day's plan in this book, and work in your notebook.

Thought for the Day: The goodness in my soul knows no size or weight.

When you choose not to be bulimic, you also choose to change your values. Probably you have been prejudiced against the way you look or how much you weigh. We have been encouraging you to love and trust your inner self. Now is the time to accept your outer self. You can be loved with any body!

The Morning Warmup: Study your naked self in a mirror. While you are observing, remember that no one has an "ideal" body. Think of a lover who desires you exactly as you see your reflection.

Today's Options:
1. Gentle, stretching exercise; then a quick, short walk.
2. Go to a quiet place (a museum, church, or art gallery).
3. Call someone new from your support list.
4. Buy some clothing that fits.
5. Clean out your closet.

Homework: Day 12
1. List some "happy couples" you know. Are they in love? Do you think they have a good sexual relationship? Do they have "ideal" bodies?

2. Go to a shopping area and observe people. What do they look like? Does anyone have an "ideal" body? Do smaller people seem happier than larger people? Are there people eating-on-the-run? Are they happy? Does anyone judge your appearance? Record some observations and thoughts.

3. Make a list of 5-10 myths and 5-10 rules that you want to change. A myth may be something like, "Skinny people are happier." A rule may be something like, "I can't eat ice cream at night, because I'll gain weight."

4. Read a book with a feminist topic.

Good night: You can think about the past, but *right now* is what is real. This moment is what you're experiencing. Let go of the past. Old concepts don't work anymore. You can dream of a better future, but it will only come true if you strive towards that dream today.

DAY 13
Clean-up Time!

You have made a strong commitment to ending your bulimia, especially if you are still following this program. Put extra effort into the course for these last two days. You are paving the way for your future.

First Things First: Read the Thought for the Day, do the Morning Warmup, read the entire day's plan in this book, and make a short journal entry.

Thought for the Day: I can make small changes with big results!

You have to change some things about your environment in order to support the changes in yourself. Notice details.

The Morning Warmup: Do a music appreciation activity. Some ideas: listen with headphones to your favorite song, play an instrument, sing, or dance.

Short Journal Entry: Write a summary of what you've learned in your study project, then reflect on your feelings about it, such as: accomplishment, intellectual fulfillment, interest, etc.

Today's Options:

1. If you have not already done so, get rid of your scale.
2. Put an unsigned classified ad in the personals column of your newspaper that says, "I am quitting bulimia! I placed this ad instead of bingeing. I am proud of myself!"
3. Put a picture of yourself in a spot you would normally reserve for a loved one. Place flowers beside it.
4. Donate money to charity.

Homework: Day 13

1. List 10-20 things which permit your bulimia, and imagine changes. These aspects of your environment may include the usual times or places you binge, friends who are negative influences, rituals, etc. (For example: If you binge while driving to work, you can take a bus or car pool.)

2. If there is someone from your original support list whom you've resisted telling about your recovery from bulimia, talk to them today or think about why.

3. Tell someone you love them. Look in the mirror and tell yourself!

4. Work on your study project.

Good night: Not everyone who reads this book will do or even attempt to do this program. Many people may be attracted to the title, "A Two-Week Program to Stop Bingeing," but will shy away from actually "doing" anything. Regardless or whether or not you have binged, if you have followed this course for almost two weeks, you have accomplished a great feat. Think back to some of the fun moments, happy thoughts, and special places. Pleasant dreams.

DAY 14
Graduation Day!

Today is Graduation Day, and you should be quite proud of yourself. Hum "Pomp and Circumstance" (the graduation tune) to yourself all day. As with most education, graduating means new challenges, independence, and some uncertainty. By doing this program, you have progressed far in your recovery from bulimia, and now we ask you to reach ever farther. Bulimia will get more and more distant from your thoughts and consciousness as long as you keep making an effort.

First Things First: Read the Thought for the Day, do the Morning Warmup, read the entire day's plan in this book.

Thought for the Day: I have accomplished something big!

If you have followed—or even read through—this two-week program, you have seen that you have many abilities that were obscured by your food problem.

Let's summarize some of the things that you have done in this course. You've set goals, taken initiative, examined feelings about your family, laughed, learned something new, been honest and open with others, relaxed, looked at your own values, felt sexual, identified wants, made affirmations, practiced eating without bingeing, and expressed love.

Have pride inside, your horizons are limitless.

The Morning Warmup: Read through the past thirteen Morning Warmups, and remember your experiences doing them. Do these kinds of activities every morning. Today, do any that you particularly liked.

Today's Options:

1. Visit a preschool. Look at the children. You, too, are starting fresh.

2. Put binge food in a bag and drive over it with your car.

3. Plant a tree in honor of your graduation.

4. Go somewhere with your journal and make a list of all the things you have done in the last two weeks to not binge.

Homework: Day 14

1. What are your goals for the next few days, weeks, months, and year?

2. Review the course goals that you set on Day 2, and reflect on which were reached.

3. Read through your notebook.

4. Create your own program for the next week. Set goals for yourself, list options, continue accepting support, and plan some activities.

5. Final reminder: Try some form of professional therapy.

Good night: We're nostalgic writing this final message to you. We have shared our selves, hoping that you will be motivated in your recovery. Think of us cheering you on while you continue making progress. With all our hearts, we wish you love, happiness, and freedom from bulimia.

We'd like to hear from you!

Nothing has given us greater satisfaction or has touched our hearts more than the beautiful letters we have received from people who have read our books. You can write to us care of Gürze Books (B2), P.O. Box 2238, Carlsbad, CA 92018.

CHAPTER 9

A Guide for Support Groups

The format that we present here takes a group from conception through six meetings, and provides a framework for future sessions. These guidelines have been adopted for use by many professional therapists and self-led bulimia groups. Even if you do not participate in a support group, these agendas contain topics and exercises which can be useful to you. This chapter may be duplicated for group use.

Forming the Group

There are ongoing support groups throughout the United States and Canada, which can be found by contacting local treatment facilities, hospitals, or college health or counseling centers. "Overeaters Anonymous" serves this function for many people. Additionally, the eating disorder organizations listed in the back of this book may be able to help you find a local group.

We recommend professionally-led groups; but, as a last resort, you can use the guidelines in this section to start your own group. That means taking the initiative to gather members.

Classified advertising in a college or local newspaper might get enough responses to fill a group. Here's how you might word the ad:

Stop your binge/vomiting. Join a free bulimia support group. Forming now to start (the date). Confidential! Call me, (Your first name and phone number).

An advertisement such as this costs less than a binge. If you run the ad a few times, there should be plenty of people interested (5-10 is a good size). Another good way to advertise for members is to place leaflets on bulletin boards in office buildings or on college campuses. Neatly present the same basic information as above on a sheet which may be photocopied. You may want to include your phone number on tear-off tabs at the bottom of the sheet.

Arrange for the first meeting, and after that, your responsibilities as leader are over.

Rules of the Group

We have devised a basic framework for support groups, which is intended to maintain a balance of order and positive reinforcement for the participants. Professionally-led groups can dispense with most of these structural technicalities, but they can still use the basic ideas and activities that follow in the six agendas.

At the first meeting, review the following rules:

1.   Any of these rules may be changed by consensus of the group. Consensus means that everyone agrees or agrees not to stop the mutual decision of the others.

2.   The underlying issue for most bulimics is not food; therefore, the following subjects should not monopolize the discussions: diets, food, bingeing, weight control, etc.

3. Each group will follow the same basic format: introduction and goals, discussion, exercises, and summary. The topics and exercises will be provided here.

4. At each meeting, different people must be appointed to the following jobs, which may be rotated:

- facilitator (group leader to introduce each topic and call on people to speak)
- time-keeper (to keep on schedule)
- gripe-control monitor (to interrupt anyone who is monopolizing the focus)

5. At the beginning of each meeting, the agenda will be reviewed and anyone who wants to add an item may do so.

6. One requirement of all group members is complete honesty.

7. No meeting shall end on a pessimistic or depressed note. If these conditions exist at the scheduled close, then a discussion or activity must be enacted to uplift the spirit of the group.

First Meeting Agenda

1. Review the rules of the group.

2. Appoint facilitator, time-keeper, and gripe-control monitor. These positions might not be necessary in professionally-led groups.

3. The facilitator reviews this agenda with the group, and agenda items are added. Approximate times are allocated for each item.

4. **Introduction:** Everyone in the group introduces themselves and explains why they have joined the group. (Keep these introductions to a couple of minutes each.)

5. **Discussion:** This meeting's topic is about the nature of support. To begin the discussion, each member of the group takes turns answering the following questions:

• Who has been supportive of your recovery, and what have they done that has been helpful?

• If anyone else knows about your bulimia, how did they react when they found out, and how did that make you feel?

• What are a few do's and don'ts you would recommend to a support person to better help you?

• What will you offer to other members of the group to support them?

After everyone has spoken, the group can have an open discussion about some of the things that came out in the exercise. This is not to psychoanalyze each other, but to gain insight through each other's disclosures. (20-40 minutes).

6. **Exercise:** RELAXATION! (15-20 minutes)

Everyone gets into a comfortable position, either sitting or lying down. One person talks the others through the following exercise in a quiet monotone, while the others relax with their eyes closed. Here is the exercise:

Take three deep breaths, inhaling, holding the breath, and exhaling to the count of ten (one-two-three... inhale, one-two-three... holding, one-two-three... exhaling). Afterwards, breathe normally. As you inhale, feel as though you are being filled with light; and as you exhale, empty yourself of stress. Feel your body relax. Concentrate on your toes, relax them. Continue this, relaxing your feet, ankles, calves, knees, etc., until every part of the body is mentioned. Feel yourself filled with light and health, goodness, purity, contentment, power, etc. Remain in this state for several minutes before slowly reviving.

7. **Summary:** The group needs to set a time and place for the next meeting. It can be as soon as tomorrow! Because this is a support group, a commitment needs to be made by the

members to come to at least the next meeting, with the intent of coming to all six. Exchange phone numbers so that individuals can use each other for support outside of the group.

A Few Words About Your Progress: This first meeting may have been difficult for you. Opening up with your feelings may not have been easy or even possible. Give yourself some time; it will get easier. Individual or group therapy, medical examinations, and other steps towards self-help that are suggested in this book should be made in addition to the support group. In any case, stick to your commitment to coming to the next meeting.

Second Meeting Agenda

1. If appropriate, appoint a new facilitator, time-keeper, and gripe-control monitor.

2. Review the guidelines of the group and agenda.

3. **Introduction:** "I wish...," "I want...," and "I am..."

Everyone takes a few minutes to think about their answers to the above sentences within the context of recovery issues. Then, take turns giving answers for "I wish . . ." until everyone has had a chance to answer two or three times (For example: "I wish I had better communication with my father.") The same is done for "I want . . ." and "I am . . ." (IMPORTANT: Try to be positive with your language. For example, instead of "I am a binger," say, "I am learning to stop myself from binge eating.")

4. **Discussion:** This meeting's topic is "Family Relations." Each group member takes five uninterrupted minutes to describe their family. It may be helpful to address areas such as how your family relates, your parents' characters, and family meals. After everyone has had a chance to speak, open the floor to discussion and questions. Listen carefully! Try to understand some of the reasons for your eating behavior.

5. **Exercise:** ASSERTIVENESS TO MOM OR DAD!

For the first part of this exercise, everyone writes some things that they dislike about one parent (living or dead, past or present). Then, take turns sharing answers, and continue until everyone has spoken two or three times. This exercise is then done again—this time stressing the parents' likable traits. This is continued until everyone has spoken at least three times. (Example: "I dislike how financially dependent my mother acts," and "I like that my mom listens when I talk to her.")

The second part of this exercise is a gripe session with mother or father. Get in pairs or triads and take turns spending about ten minutes in role-playing that allows you to assert yourself to your parent(s). You may bring up old wounds that have never healed, you may scream, or you may try to explain your feelings. Express your true self in a way that you have always wished you could when speaking to your actual parents. Even though this is only a role-play, try to be serious and avoid hiding your feelings. When playing the parent role, try to put yourself fully into that person's character.

6. **Relaxation:** Take five minutes for group relaxation, led by a volunteer. This can be as simple as sitting silently with eyes closed.

7. Set a time and place for the next meeting.

8. Share a few words about commitment to the group. Group members must be able to rely on each other for support inside and outside of the meetings.

Do not procrastinate working on your individual steps towards getting better. If you need to seek professional therapy, have a medical examination, tell more people about your bulimia, or whatever—DO IT!

Third Meeting Agenda

1. If appropriate, appoint a new facilitator, time-keeper, and gripe-control monitor.

2. Review the guidelines of the group and agenda.

3. **Introduction:** Each person spends a few minutes sharing a success story about how they have stopped themselves from bingeing. If you don't have a success story, say so, and suggest something you might try to do instead of bingeing in the future. It's important to be honest!

4. **Discussion:** This meeting's topics are "ritual" and "secrecy." Most bulimics are secretive about their food obsessions and engage in private rituals involving scales, mirrors, clothing, or food. They may even compulsively lie and steal. Each person should take a few minutes to reveal some of their secrets and answer questions. (For example: "Every time I close the bathroom door, I automatically check myself in the mirror." or "I shoplift cosmetics.") By disclosing secrets, you take away some of the importance you have given them.

5. **Exercise:** VISUALIZATION

Repeat the initial progressive relaxation technique from the first meeting. Then, the narrator tells the group to imagine themselves in front of a mirror, and to think about how they would look as a different race, a child, an old person, very ugly, the opposite sex, very beautiful, fat, thin, perfect, and finally, as light without form. (The narrator might suggest these possibilities one at a time, pausing for reflection before continuing to the next description.) Then instruct the group to visualize themselves stepping through the mirror and feeling absorbed by that light, filled with health, purity, love, contentment. Remain in that state for a few minutes before slowly reviving.

6. **Summary:** Discuss the effectiveness of the group. How can it be improved? What are everyone's feelings about the

group? Are people willing to commit to attend through the next three guided meetings? Does the group then want to: continue, disband, enlist a therapist (if there is not one already), etc. Start making plans now.

7. Set a time and place for the next meeting.

Fourth Meeting Agenda

1. If appropriate, appoint a new facilitator, time-keeper, and gripe-control monitor.

2. Review the guidelines and agenda.

3. **Introduction:** Each person shares a brief story about a positive step towards their recovery they have done or experienced since starting the support group. This may be an action, thought, or feeling.

4. **Discussion:** "The Media, Feminism, and Food."

This is an open-ended discussion. Try to keep comments related to personal experiences. Consider these questions:

• Why are bulimics mainly women?

• How does the media affect your body image?

• Why is there competition between women over their appearance?

• What role do men play in perpetuating negative stereotypes about women?

5. **Exercise:** EQUALITY

Every person takes turns changing an ad that is demeaning towards women into a non-sexist presentation. For example, the diet soft drink ad showing thin women taking their clothes off would be more honest if men and women of all colors and sizes were were equally portrayed. Also, do we really need diet drinks?

6. **Discuss the future of the group.** There are still two more meeting agendas provided here. What are everyone's

feelings about the group? Are people willing to attend those additional guided meetings? What direction is the group going to take. Is the group open to new members? A decision should be reached by the next meeting. Set a time and place.

7. **Summary:** What can we do as individuals on a daily basis to improve our self-image?

Fifth Meeting Agenda

1. If appropriate, appoint a new facilitator, time-keeper, and gripe-control monitor.

2. Review the guidelines of the group and agenda.

3. **Introduction:** Each person shares a positive experience they have had with self-help ideas or professional therapy.

4. **Discussion:** "Feelings are not good or bad, they just are."

Bulimics are often "people pleasers" who tend to keep their real feelings hidden. They are said to "swallow their feelings" instead of being honest about them. To get this discussion started, go around the group and name many kinds of feelings (happiness, fear, excitement, etc.). Then, discuss the following topics or others that develop:

• How can we identify feelings as they happen rather than hiding from them?

• What are some specific ways to handle difficult feelings?

• What is so scary about expressing feelings?

5. **Exercise:** RESPONSES TO FEELINGS

Fill in this sentence and repeat the exercise several times: "When I feel _____ , I _____ ." When there are negative responses to feelings, suggest alternatives.

6. **Summary:** Resolve the group's future. This is a good time to consider inviting a trained therapist to the next meeting, if that has not already been done.

7. Set a time and place for the next meeting.

8. Share your feelings about the group's effectiveness.

Sixth Meeting Agenda

1. Appoint a new facilitator, time-keeper, and gripe-control monitor.

2. Review the guidelines of the group and agenda.

3. **Introduction:** In what positive ways have you changed since joining the group? Everyone takes a turn answering.

4. **The Future of the Group:** If your group's future is uncertain at this time, determining its future is a top priority. Spend as much time as needed to finish up this matter. Work together to develop discussion topics and exercises if there are going to be more meetings.

5. **Discussion:** This meeting's topic is "Intimacy." Bulimics are afraid of being in relationships. They are afraid to express opinions or that they might inconvenience others with their needs. They think everyone disapproves of them. Take turns answering the following questions, and discuss the answers:

• What good qualities can you bring to a friendship?

• What makes you think people automatically dislike you?

• Is there anyone with whom you can be completely yourself?

• Do you want to work towards intimacy with any group members, in or out of meetings?

6. **Exercise:** SUPPORT

Sit in a circle holding hands. With your eyes closed, take three deep breaths. After the last breath, silently express thanks for everyone's sharing and support. Remain quiet for five minutes.

CHAPTER 10

Resources

About Our Surveys

We conducted two surveys of people recovered and recovering from bulimia and other forms of "problem eating." The first, in 1983, was answered by 214 women and three men, and the second was in 1991, with 152 women and three men. Each questionnaire included factual questions (sex, age, the number of years with bulimia, the length of time actively seeking a recovery, etc.), and the remaining questions asked them to rank causes, recovery options, and helpful activities. These were not scientific studies, but the results provided practical answers to what works in recovery.

We also encouraged them to write short essays on subjects such as: Is hunger a physical or emotional sensation? In what ways do you relate food, body image, and sexuality? What helped you make the decision to end your food problems? What are specific things you do to stop a binge? These essays are excerpted throughout this book in *italics*.

Finally, we also sent out similar questionnaires to therapists who work in this field, and their insights are reflected throughout the text.

Again, it is with love and respect that we thank everyone who contributed to this book.

Here are some of the relevant statistics of the combined surveys. The following percentages indicates responses of 4 or 5 (on a scale of 1=small influence and 5=big influence):

"Which of these contributed to the cause of your food problems?" Guilt, shame, low self-esteem, 86%; Family life (you as child), 72%; Mental numbness, 61%; Sexual abuse, 59%; Media, 46%; Taste of food, 44%; Fear of relationships, 40%.

"Of the recovery options you've tried, rate their helpfulness." Self-help with the support of my friends and loved-ones, 84%; Professional therapy, 62%; Drug treatment, 56%; Professionally-led group, 51%; Hospitalization, 39%; Non-professionally led group, 39%; Overeaters Anonymous, 35%.

"Of those which apply, which activities have been helpful in your recovery?" Speaking honestly, 88%; Reading, 73%; Nutritional eating, 72%; Physical exercise, 64%; Spiritual pursuits, 59%; Journal writing, 48%; Lectures or seminars, 46%; Relaxation techniques, 34%; Making lists, 31%.

One of the most interesting facets of the surveys was the diversity of the respondents:

Age: Average age, 32; mean age, 31; youngest, 12; oldest, 63; 84% were in their 20s and 30s

Stage of the problem: Recovered for many years, in recovery, just starting to look at their problem, "hopelessly food addicted," and everything in-between including a 63 year-old "compulsive binge-eater since adolescence."

Professions include: Nurse, truck driver, therapist, social worker, nutritionist, parent, grandparent, secretary, geneticist, accountant, professor, executive director, waitress, minister, student, librarian, computer programmer, ESL teacher, doctor of naturopathy, cosmetologist, photographer, musician, fish factory worker, college director of counseling, gymnastics coach, paralegal, and psychotherapist!

Ethnic/Religious: American Indian, Caucasian, Black, Brethern, Latino, Oriental; Agnostic, Atheist, Bahai, Baptist, Catholic, Christian, Episcopalian, Evangelical Christian, Jehovah's Witness, Jewish, Lutheran, Mennonite, Methodist, Presbyterian, Protestant, Unitarian Universalist, Zen Buddhist.

Family background: "Filthy rich," upper-middle class, middle class, poor, matriarchal, patriarchal, single-parent, traditional, abusive, controlling, incestuous, strict, permissive, perfectionistic!

Obviously, people with eating disorders come from all walks of life.

Further Reading

In earlier versions of *Bulimia: A Guide to Recovery*, we included a reading list, but doing so had disadvantages. Quite often, we got calls from people who could not find books we recommended. Also, our reading list could not keep up with the numbers of new books being written about eating disorders and related issues.

In 1986, we put together a catalogue of twenty relevant books on eating disorders. Since then, the *Gürze Eating Disorders Bookshelf Catalogue* has become the most comprehensive source for literature on this subject. It offers photos and descriptions of more than 125 current books and tapes.

For a FREE copy, use the order form in the back of this book or contact: Gürze Books, P.O. Box 2238, Carlsbad, CA 92018, phone (800) 434-7533.

National Eating Disorders Organizations

There are many national and local organizations devoted to helping people who have eating disorders. They typically offer written materials, bibliographies, newsletters, and often have referral services or sponsor support groups. Here we list some of the largest, nonprofit organizations. These are all national, but many have local chapters:

AABA
American Anorexia/Bulimia Assoc.
133 Cedar Lane
Teaneck, NJ 07666
(201) 836-1800

ABC
Anorexia, Bulimia, Care, Inc.
Box 213
Lincoln Center, MA 01773
(617) 259-9767

ANAD
Anorexia Nervosa and
Associated Disorders
P.O. Box 7
Highland Park, IL 60035
(312) 831-3438

ANRED
Anorexia Nervosa and
Related Eating Disorders
P.O. Box 5102
Eugene, OR 97405
(503) 344-1144

EDAP
Eating Disorders Awareness
and Prevention
Box 2238
Carlsbad, CA 92018
(619) 434-7533

F.E.E.D.
Foundation for Education
about Eating Disorders
P.O. Box 16375
Baltimore, MD 21210
(410) 467-1074

IAEDP
International Assoc. of Eating
Disorders Professionals
123 NW 13th St. #206
Boca Raton, FL 33432-1618
(800) 800-8126

NAAS
National Anorexic Aid Society
5796 Karl Road
Columbus, OH 43229
(614) 436-1112

OA
Overeaters Anonymous
Headquarters
World Services Office
2190 West 190th St.
Torrance, CA 90504
(213) 320-7941

Index

Lindsey Hall & Leigh Cohn
(photo by Kathy Loh)

About the Authors

In 1980, Lindsey Hall and her husband, Leigh Cohn, wrote a booklet about her recovery from the binge-purge syndrome. *Eat Without Fear* was the first publication solely about bulimia, and later was expanded with additional information into the book, *Bulimia: A Guide to Recovery.*

Lindsey and Leigh have also written a number of other books, including *Self-Esteem Tools for Recovery* and *Dear Kids of Alcoholics.* They edit *The Gürze Eating Disorders Bookshelf Catalogue,* a comprehensive selection of books and tapes. Their works have been used in thousands of homes, colleges, high schools, hospitals, and by professional therapists throughout the world.

Lindsey graduated from Stanford University with a degree in Psychology. She is President-elect of Eating Disorders Awareness and Prevention, a non-profit association which sponsors the annual "Eating Disorders Awareness Week." Leigh earned an M.A.T. in English Education from Northwestern University, is Executive Editor of *Eating Disorders: The Journal of Treatment and Prevention,* and is President of Publishers Marketing Association, a non-profit trade association.

Lindsey and Leigh are happily married and have two sons, Neil and Charlie. They are honored that their projects help people become more self-fulfilled and loving.

Also from Gürze Books

FREE:
The Gürze Eating Disorders Bookshelf Catalogue

This catalogue includes more than 125 books, tapes, and videos on eating disorders and related topics. It is used as a resource by therapists, educators, and other health care professionals. The subjects include bulimia, anorexia nervosa, compulsive eating, obesity, body image, nutrition, wellness, sexual abuse recovery, the history and politics of thinness and beauty, self-esteem, and more.

Understanding Bulimia (audio tape)
Lindsey Hall & Leigh Cohn

This recording provides a revealing look at this usually secretive food obsession. Hall describes how her "diet" became an obsession, that she used it as a substitute for relationships and sexuality, her methods of bingeing and vomiting, how she recovered, and why she is healthy, happy, and free from food fears. She is a personable, engaging speaker.

Self-Esteem Tools for Recovery
Lindsey Hall & Leigh Cohn

This book helps readers experience their innermost selves, the source of true self-esteem. It speaks directly to people who have decided that their coping mechanisms no longer serve them as lifestyles. Included are short, specific tools, easy-to-use exercises, and pertinent examples to help readers gain confidence in making decisions, make peace with the past, overcome destructive thoughts and behavior, and live in a state of love and compassion.

Father Hunger: Fathers, Daughters & Food
Margo Maine, Ph.D.

"Father Hunger" is the emptiness experienced by women whose fathers were emotionally absent, a void that leads to unrealistic body image, yo-yo dieting, food fears, and disordered eating patterns. "Father Hunger" is a common phenomenon of Western culture, whose dictates and myths limit a father's role, creating a loss for all family members.

Dr. Maine discusses practical solutions to help readers understand and improve their father/daughter relationships and help families reconnect as well.

My Name is Caroline
Caroline Adams Miller

In this shocking confession, Caroline illustrates how her picture-perfect life was a cover-up for bulimia. The gripping prose is a compelling description of her thoughts and experiences as well as relationships with her husband, parents, and support group members. Caroline's triumphant recovery process is inspiring reading for anyone struggling with an eating disorder.

Dear Kids of Alcoholics
Lindsey Hall & Leigh Cohn

This is an honest, helpful, hopeful book for young readers to better understand alcoholism in the family. Children (ages 8-16) will identify with the feelings of its main character, Jason, a boy who explains facts about alcoholism with touching stories about his dad's sensitivity to alcohol, destructive behavior, and recovery process. It is illustrated and has an accompanying guidebook for counselors, educators, and parents.

Order Form

I have enclosed a check for _____ . *Please send me:*

_____ FREE copies of the *Eating Disorders Bookshelf Catalogue*

_____ Copies of *Bulimia: A Guide to Recovery - Revised Edition*
$11.95 each - 5 or more copies @ $9.95

_____ Copies of *Understanding Bulimia (90 min. audio tape)*
$11.95 each - 5 or more copies @ $9.95

_____ Copies of *Self-Esteem Tools for Recovery*
$9.95 each - 5 or more copies @ $7.50

_____ Copies of *Father Hunger: Fathers, Daughters & Food*
$12.95 each - 5 or more copies @ $10.50

_____ Copies of *My Name is Caroline*
$12.95 each - 5 or more copies @ $10.50

_____ Copies of *Dear Kids of Alcoholics*
$6.95 each - 5 or more copies @ $5.50

_____ Copies of *Dear Kids of Alcoholics - Guidebook*
$4.95 each - 5 or more copies @ $3.95

Shipping & Handling: $1.95 @ one copy, $.95 ea. @ 2-9 copies
$.75 each @ 10 or more copies

California residents add 7.75% sales tax.

NAME _____

ADDRESS _____

CITY/ST/ZIP _____

PHONE _____

Send a copy of this order form and payment to:
Gürze Books (B2) • P.O. Box 2238 • Carlsbad, CA 92018

Phone orders accepted: (800) 756-7533